To J.C.
Without whom this would not have been possible.

*"Uncertainty affects all of us and
influences practically everything in our lives."*
Brent Nelson Ph. D.

THE
THEORY OF
EVERYTHING

How uncertainty creates the world in which we live.

BRENT NELSON PH. D.

HH

Heather Hill

Cover Art BNelson

Table of Contents

Preface

I have a theory....

Theory is one of the most misused words in the English language. When people say, "I have a theory" what they are really describing is an observation, assumption, or hypothesis.

But, "I have a hypothesis," doesn't sound as cool as saying "I have a theory."

A theory is a way to explain how something works based upon research. We use theory to help us better understand ourselves, others, and the world around us.

Science looks to form an elegant unified theory of physics, nature, and the properties of matter and energy, sometimes referred to as "the theory of everything." But has yet to unify the theories of how the physical world works.

However, most people are not concerned with this world created by nature. They have to deal with a social world created by people.

We live in a world of our own creation. From our homes, to our workplaces, to how we behave and communicate with one another, much of the world in which we live is socially created. Even how we understand the physical world itself.

This book is about how uncertainty motivates our behavior and how we communicate with one another. It has unified the laws that govern behavioral communicating to form an elegant *Grand Unified Theory of Everything*.

This book is about how uncertainty motivates us to create the world in which we live. A world that is socially constructed through our communicating with one another.

This book describes how things come into being. How ideas become reality. How people form relationships. How organizations grow and become successful only to wither and die. And how societies become great, only to fall.

So, how is our social world created? What was the Big Bang event that set off a chain reaction that affects how we behave and communicate today? What are the forces that affect all of us each and every day?

We were created with needs and wants we cannot fulfill ourselves. How these are fulfilled creates uncertainty. This means that uncertainty has motivated our behavior since the beginning of time.

Throughout history, most of human activity has been motivated by uncertainty. Yet, never before have so many people experienced so much uncertainty.

The last two centuries have seen more advancement in our quality of life than ever before. Society has made great advancements to reduce uncertainty, but it has likely made us more vulnerable to uncertainty.

The most pivotal events in recent history were rooted in uncertainty and increased worldwide uncertainty to unprecedented levels. These events included Y2K, terrorism, wars, earthquakes, hurricanes, tsunamis, oil spills, nuclear disaster, and the financial crisis with falling home prices, bank failures, bankruptcies, and the stock market crash.

Uncertainty affects all of us and is always present. It influences how we think and motivates our behavior. Understanding uncertainty can change how you think about practically everything in life. So, it is helpful to understand how uncertainty affects you and what you can do about it.

This book takes the approach of examining the nature of how people actually communicate. Typical approaches to communication focus on topics or types of communication like interpersonal, family, or organizational communication. They characterize communication based on a sender or receiver using abstract terms.

These approaches are often organized by where the communication takes place rather than the nature of how people are actually communicating, which can create artificial divisions that may not accurately reflect real life circumstances.

This book utilizes a *levels of interaction approach* to cover practically all ways that we communicate. This provides a means to examine how we communicate in a comprehensive way to avoid duplication or omission of information.

This book is written in a casual, conversational style as if someone was talking with you. It is written for ease of reading using informal language with minimal technical jargon or academic terms. It is intended to be used by anyone without the need for any specific knowledge or skills.

In order to characterize communicating as an active continuous process, this book uses the words "communicating" or "communicate" rather than "communication." This is meant to emphasize communicating as an active and dynamic process that occurs between people rather than communication, which can seem more passive or static. Communicating begins with one individual person and as the reader of this book that person is you.

Communicating is how we reduce uncertainty, share meaning, and invest in ourselves and others through the exchange of verbal and nonverbal information. Communicating is how we share our experiences, get to know other people, and learn about ourselves, others, and the world around us. Understanding how communicating works is helpful to improving our quality of life and is an essential skill for our career.

Communicating effectively is important because of the amount of time we spend communicating. It is how we gain information and new ideas, learn how to do things, and learn about ourselves and the world around us.

Through communicating we develop our own identity and self-concept to facilitate personal growth. It is how we show that we support and care about others, and create and maintain many types of relationships.

This book is written to help you to increase your awareness and provide you with options, so you can determine what works best for you. It does not advocate a specific course of action because there is no best approach that works for everyone all of the time. This book is not meant to provide professional advice.

This book can be used as a course textbook, or supplementary resource for schools, businesses, groups, and organizations. Research in this book was utilized in new and creative ways to determine the effectiveness of how people communicate to share meaning with one another.

This book utilizes scholarly research for the purpose of reporting, commentary, analysis, and criticism to create new knowledge and insights into behavioral communicating. The methods of gathering information utilized in this book include observation and experience through the process of naturalistic observation as a research methodology.

Much of what we know comes from personal experience gathered through our five senses. If we want to know about something we may observe what others do, listen to them talk about their experiences, or participate ourselves.

For instance, if we want to learn how to play tennis we might read about it or observe how others do it. We may take lessons from someone more experienced and we practice doing it to improve our skills.

Naturalistic observation is a scientific methodology that facilitates understanding of how things work through observation and participation in the natural environment. This allows analysis of communicative behaviors in naturally occurring groups subject to real life influences.

This method produces findings that can be more useful than forming artificial groups with contrived tasks that can make universal generalizations problematic. This method ensures that participants behave in ways that are more applicable to actual situations and that the findings are not based on any particular individual, group, or set of behaviors.

This method of gaining knowledge is similar to how we learn much of what we know. We process and analyze information to look for findings that can be useful to us.

Observation gives us an objective view as an outsider, whereas with naturalistic observation we can share experiences and gain the knowledge of an insider to better understand what we observe.

Naturalistic observation, interviews, focus groups, and seminars provided the basis of the knowledge utilized herein. This method provides a way that you can get to know more about yourself, others, and the world around you. This can be an ongoing process that continues throughout our lives.

The author of this book is the first person to develop and apply new and innovative methodologies to understand how people are motivated by laws that govern communicating and behavior.

The author of this book is the first person to identify these laws, *The Nelsonian Laws of Uncertainty, Shared Meaning, and Investing*, which comprise a *Grand Unified Theory of Behavioral Communication*. These laws have influenced people's behavior since the beginning of time.

Uncertainty affects all of us and influences practically everything in our lives. Uncertainty is difficult to cover in one book and could be studied indefinitely.

This book focuses on how uncertainty affects how we communicate and our behavior. While this book is designed to be comprehensive, it is not meant to be all encompassing.

This book is not meant to be the last word on uncertainty. It is meant to increase awareness in order to provide a place to initiate a discussion of how uncertainty affects us all.

Uncertainty has a larger, more important function, it can affect who we are as an individual and what kind of person we want to be. It can determine who we are as a people and what kind of society we want to be.

At one time the world we live in did not exist. It was how people communicated in the past that created the world we live in today. It is how we communicate today that will determine what kind of world future generations will live in tomorrow.

Chapter 1
The Theory of Everything

How do you know what you know? How do you know what is true? In the past the most brilliant minds developed knowledge that they believed to be true, which we now know is not. Consider that a second century astronomer determined that the Sun and all the planets revolved around the Earth.

In Medieval times, it was thought that alchemy could turn lead into gold. In Colonial times, some women were thought to be witches. More recently, it was thought that cigarettes had health benefits because they were both a stimulant and relaxant.

So, how do we know that what we believe today is true? How do we know what we consider to be true today might be proven to be not true in the future? Since people create knowledge, this raises an important question. If enough people decide that something is right, does that make it right? Some societies thought that human sacrifices or the burning of witches was right. So, what are we doing today that we consider right because some people perceive it's right, but may not be in the future?

How a society creates and disseminates knowledge can determine how they solve problems to fulfill their needs and wants. Throughout history people of different cultures from different geographic regions had similar experiences, faced similar problems, and accomplished similar tasks. They often had the same needs and wants that they sought to fulfill. Even though they have many similarities, they developed distinctly different solutions often based upon their own unique social reality.

So, how do we come to know what we know? We all have our own way of obtaining information to know what we know. Much of what we know we learn through our education and experiences. This can make it difficult to change what people already know because they may resist new information, perhaps even becoming defensive.

Rather than trying to convince them to change what they know, challenge them to think beyond what they know to gain new knowledge. This can help motivate people to think beyond what they perceive as true. People may resist changing what they believe to be true, but they are less likely to want to be perceived as being unwilling to learn something new. Do they feel that they already know everything there is to know, so they don't need to know anything new?

When we want to know something, how do we find out about it? We might ask others who have experience. We might look to the past to see how it was done before. We may look to forces larger than ourselves to gain inspiration through spiritual revelation. Some societies gained knowledge from sacred texts that looked to the knowledge of the past. We may look at what's available to us in the present using methods like trial and error. We could utilize the scientific method to create new knowledge in the future.

We create knowledge in these ways to help us understand the world around us.
• Perceiving. Gaining knowledge through our five senses; sight, sound, touch, taste, and smell.
• Doing. Gaining knowledge through experience by participating.
• Thinking. Gaining knowledge through education, rationality, logic, or scientific inquiry.
• Believing. Gaining knowledge through religion or faith by trusting in something unseen.
• Realizing. Gaining knowledge through instinct or revelation.
• Feeling. Gaining knowledge through intuition, emotions, or empathy.

Knowledge is not just about how we gain information, it's also about how we use it. Gaining new knowledge utilizes a process where we select, organize, and interpret information to give it meaning so it fits in with what we already know. How this happens is influenced by uncertainty. When we feel uncertainty, we are more likely to be open to new knowledge.

When uncertainty is reduced, people can feel more sure about themselves and what they are doing, so they may not be open to new ideas or different ways of thinking or doing things. When someone is overly certain, they are not necessarily open to other ideas. Throughout history, many people were certain about things they believed to be true that were not, which sometimes had disastrous consequences.

What if?

What if you found yourself in a place that was unfamiliar to you, that you knew nothing about? What if you were surrounded by people you did not know, who you could not communicate with or understand? What would you do?

While this is unlikely to happen, it is similar to what we experience when we are born. We are born with little understanding of ourselves, others, and the world around us. We are born into a world we did not create, that we know nothing about.

We are surrounded by people we cannot clearly communicate with or understand. We are totally dependent upon them for all of our needs to live. This motivates us to start a lifelong process of developing communicating skills, so we can better understand ourselves, others, and the world around us.

At some time in the distant past, humans began to explore a planet they knew little about. They encountered things and had experiences they sought to understand.

They experienced a high degree of uncertainty that motivated them to try to reduce it in order to fulfill their needs and wants. They had to develop ways of communicating with one another to better understand themselves, other people, and the world around them.

This book is about the process by which we learn about ourselves, others, and the world around us. It is about how our needs and wants motivate us to communicate with others. It is about how we share our experiences to create meaning. It is about how uncertainty has motivated practically all of human activity throughout history.

This process of gaining understanding through communicating has worked over time to advance human society. Practically everything we do, everything we think, everything we learn, everything we experience, and everything we know is created and shared by communicating with other people. The history of human civilization is the process of gaining and sharing a better understanding of ourselves, others, and the world around us in order to reduce uncertainty.

Needs and Wants

Uncertainty begins with how we were created. As human beings we are all born with needs we cannot fulfill ourselves, so they must be fulfilled by others in order for us to survive. When we are born our needs are fulfilled by adults like our parents and family. We have to learn to communicate our needs to others who try to understand them. Having needs that must be fulfilled motivates a lifelong process of communicating with others.

As children, we develop additional needs and discover that we want more. Since we are still dependent on our parents and others to fulfill our needs and wants, we are motivated to develop ways of communicating in order to get what we want. For example, a young child may want a toy and if they do not get it, they may go to great lengths including crying and throwing a tantrum to communicate how much they want it.

As we get older we have an ever increasing number of needs and wants. What constitutes a need or want depends upon many things. It depends upon who we are, where we live, what we do, our family, our culture, our experiences, and our traditions. We might feel that we need to have what we see others have. While our basic human needs remain the same, other needs and wants are constantly changing over time. We may feel we need to have something and once we get it we may decide we no longer want it.

We can have potentially unlimited wants that are constrained by limited resources. We can feel tension between competing needs because we may not have the resources to fulfill them all. In relationships, competing needs can create tension and even conflict between people who have different ideas on how resources should be utilized. We have many needs and wants we cannot fulfill by ourselves, so we are motivated to communicate with others to fulfill them.

For example, in order to provide for ourselves and our family we need an income, which motivates us to find a job where we have to communicate with our boss and coworkers. This makes our ability to fulfill our needs and wants to some extent contingent upon our ability to communicate with other people.

There are some needs that are required for survival, however, other needs are contingent upon each individual person. Some people need to be around others or be the center of attention, where others need time to themselves.

Everyone is different with their own priorities for fulfilling their needs and wants, so there is no one way that everyone organizes or prioritizes their needs and wants. It all depends upon our individual priorities. Needs do not form a hierarchy like a video game where each person has to satisfy one level in order to proceed to the next. We choose which ones are important to fulfill and which ones are not.

Self fulfillment or self actualization is not about fulfilling our needs in a predetermined order, but instead being able to pursue the ones that are important to us and being able to put aside others which are not.

We each have complementary and conflicting needs and wants that can motivate our behavior. So, it can be problematic to attempt to simplify how these work by creating a single, simplistic metaphor. Life cannot, and should not, be trivialized as a form of game playing with winners and losers. It is much more complex and sophisticated than that. These terms carry generalized stereotypical positive and negative connotations that can potentially limit their significance and application.

For example, some people might choose not to play or they make up their own rules. Not everyone benefits by winning and some benefit by losing. Even the definitions of these terms are relative based on individual interpretation making generalized comparisons or application problematic.

How our individual needs and wants motivate behavior in order to reduce uncertainty cannot easily be generalized as there is no one best one size fits all approach that works for everyone in all situations. It is unlikely that people play individual separate games resulting in a winner and loser, or both winners or losers. More commonly, we participate in a series of interconnected interactions were we may get some of what we want, motivating communicative behavior.

Our needs and wants have an important impact on our behavior. We communicate for a reason, which is often based on our needs and wants. Since we need other people to fulfill them, we are motivated to communicate with them to do so. In order to better understand ourselves and our behavior, it can be helpful to know more about how our needs and wants motivate our actions to communicate with others.

By being aware of our needs and wants, we can communicate more effectively to improve the quality of our relationships with other people. All too often we may not be aware of what those needs are or why they motivate our behavior. By understanding how needs and wants work to motivate our behavior and how we communicate with others, we can make choices about what we do rather than reacting without knowing why.

The nature of needs and wants.

We may feel frustration, depression, or tension in our lives and wonder why we are feeling this way. Tension is a natural part of everyday life because it arises out of our needs and wants. Unfulfilled needs and wants are uncomfortable, which creates tension. We often have more needs and wants than we have resources to fulfill, forcing us to set priorities that can be difficult because it can leave some of them unfulfilled creating tension.

Some needs and wants are mutually exclusive and cannot be fulfilled at the same time creating tension between them. Balancing tension created by our needs and wants can be one of the most challenging things we do. By having an awareness of our needs and wants, and how they motivate behavior, we can reduce our feelings of frustration and tension.

We have many conflicting needs and wants. For instance, we need to feel close to others, but we also need our own space. We need to belong to groups like our family, but we also need our own individual identity. We need safety and stability, but we also need adventure and excitement. We need to share information about ourselves to develop relationships, but we also need privacy. We need to work and be productive, but we also like to take time off and have fun.

When we have conflicting needs and wants, we might feel tension or guilt. For example, if our family wants us to spend time with them, but we need some time to ourselves, we may feel guilt or tension. By understanding how competing or conflicting needs and wants affect us, we can find a balance to avoid unnecessary frustration or tension.

How we perceive our needs and wants could be characterized in the following ways.

1. Compelling needs and wants. These motivate us to take action.
2. Competing needs and wants. These create tension between which one to choose.
3. Conflicting needs and wants. These can hinder us from taking action.

In order to better understand what motivates your behavior, make a list of your needs in order of importance. Do the same for your wants. Next to each one, on a scale of 1 to 10 write down how well you feel they have been fulfilled. Doing this can help increase your awareness of your needs and wants and how they motivate you. Not fulfilling needs and wants to meet expectations can lead to unhappiness and tension leaving us feeling frustrated and depressed, but we may not know why.

Making a list can help you determine what is important to you, so that you can allocate your time effectively to fulfill more of them. It can help you spend less time doing things that make you end up feeling frustrated and spend more time doing things that make you feel fulfilled.

We were created by nature with needs and wants we cannot fulfill ourselves. Unfulfilled needs and wants make us uncomfortable, and since we don't like being uncomfortable, we are motivated to take action to alleviate this discomfort by fulfilling them. Since it is difficult for us to fulfill all our needs and wants on our own, we are motivated to get assistance from other people. In order to do this, we must be able to communicate with them. This is how our needs and wants motivate us to communicate with one another.

When we communicate, people share stories about themselves with us which gives us a better understanding of others and adds deeper meaning to our own experiences. This process helps to create a shared understanding between people that can help to develop relationships. Developing relationships is fundamental to the formation of families, groups, organizations, and communities.

These relationships help us to create a stable society that can provide predictability, so we can know what our lives might be like in the future. This gives us confidence to invest our time, energy, money, and other resources in ourselves, our families, businesses, and society.

The Laws of Communicating

As humans we were created by nature with needs and wants. Needs that must be fulfilled in order to survive and wants that motivate us to take action to fulfill them. We could have been created by nature to be simpler and less complicated with fewer needs and wants like other creatures on earth.

We could have been created with the ability to satisfy all our needs and wants by ourselves, but this was not how nature intended us to be. We were created with complex needs and wants, so we have to take action and communicate with others in order to fulfill them. This means that the laws of communicating were created by nature because we were meant by nature to communicate and become involved with one another.

It is difficult to talk about communicating in and of itself because it is so closely linked with our behavior. Rarely do we just communicate with someone and that's the end of it. It is more common for us to communicate in the process of doing things. We don't often do things without communicating about them and we don't often communicate without taking some kind of action.

How we communicate influences our behavior and the behavior of others. Our behavior has the ability to communicate information about us to others and the behavior of other people communicates information about them to us. So, when this book refers to communicating what is actually being described is behavioral communicating.

Communicating and behavior are virtually inseparable because our behavior communicates information to others. Behavior is better understood when we know why people communicate because it gives what they do meaning. Therefore, this process can be thought of as behavioral communicating. This consists not only of how people use behavior to communicate, but how communicating affects behavior. It's about what people say and do. It's about why we do what we do.

How we communicate with other people is shaped by forces that originated in how the world was created. These forces are contained in laws that shape and motivate human behavior. The laws that influence our behavior comprise a *Grand Unified System of Communicative Behavior.* Like the laws of physics, these laws have governed human behavior and how we communicate since the beginning of time. By understanding these laws and the forces they create, we can better understand human behavior and how we communicate.

The laws of communicating are analogous to the laws of nature, like the laws of physics, because they were created by nature. They apply universally to everyone, they do not change, and they cannot be altered by people. These laws shape human behavior and how we communicate. They can be used to help understand what motivates behavior including how and why we communicate with one another.

The author of this book is the first person to develop *The Nelsonian Laws of Uncertainty, Shared Meaning, and Investing,* which comprise a *Grand Unified Theory of Behavioral Communication.* They are in order of importance because the process begins with the first law and each preceding law is created by those before it.

Uncertainty

Life is uncertain. The world around us is chaotic. Things can happen with no warning and for no apparent reason. We may know that some things might happen, but do not know when or how. No one can accurately predict the future or has the ability to control everything that might happen.

Despite our best planning things do not go as we expect. We experience things we do not want such as illness, financial troubles, and natural disasters. We are aware of our own mortality, even though we do not know when or how it will happen. All these things create uncertainty.

Uncertainty is the first and most important law of behavioral communicating because it makes the other two laws possible. It is like the law of gravity because it affects everyone and cannot be changed. No matter how much people seek to reduce uncertainty, it cannot be totally eliminated. This is in part because we have needs and wants that must be fulfilled, because there are things about life we don't know, and because there are things that are out of our control.

Even if uncertainty could be totally eliminated, it would be detrimental for us and society. The law of uncertainty provides critical functions that shape who we are as individuals. Without uncertainty we would not be motivated to do the things that need to be done for society to function.

The degree of uncertainty we each experience is based on our individual perspectives and experiences. What constitutes uncertainty for one person may be viewed as a challenge or adventure for another. Uncertainty is different for each person because it is based upon our past experiences, the degree to which our needs and wants are fulfilled, and the difference between our perceptions and expectations. Uncertainty can be viewed as the difference between how much security and stability we have in our life compared to what we need or want to have.

Uncertainty can affect our self-concept and how we interact with others based on the degree of confidence we have in ourselves and our abilities. It can be the difference between what we know and what we need or want to know. It can be the degree to which we feel we have some predictability about the future and having our expectations met. Uncertainty occurs when reality, or our perception of reality, does not meet our expectations. Uncertainty can be measured by the degree to which there is a gap between our expectations and our perception of reality.

Uncertainty should not be considered the same as confusion or inaction. Even though these words are sometimes used interchangeably, they are not the same. Confusion is a lack of clarity and indecision is the inability to make a decision. Uncertainty does not necessarily prevent us from thinking clearly or having the ability to act decisively.

When we go through times where we feel uncertain about things around us, perhaps even about ourselves, it is not necessarily uncertainty. Rather, it may come from confusion or indecision about what we should be doing because we want to know that we are doing the right thing or that our life is going in the right direction. Uncertainty is not the same as doubt, which could be considered a lack of confidence in a person's competence or ability to affect a certain outcome.

Uncertainty is not the same as a risk. Uncertainty is created by nature whereas risk is generally created by people, and we have a degree of choice over how much we risk. For example, the stock market contains uncertainty because no one can be certain what will happen to the economy or even to a particular company's stock.

The market goes up and down, the economy has growth and recession, and individual companies go through good and bad times. The more money you invest, the greater your risk because the greater your potential is for loss. However, uncertainty is unaffected by how much money you invest. If you invest $100 in a stock you have a relatively low risk because you have little to lose. If you invest $100,000 in a stock uncertainty remains the same, however, your risk has increased because you have a much greater potential for loss.

Some risk is good, we take risks to make life interesting. Greater risk often brings greater reward. Risk generally involves making choices about what is known, so we may have an idea of what we stand to lose. Uncertainty is different because it represents the unknown, we don't necessarily know what we might gain or lose.

Uncertainty reduction.

Uncertainty can be uncomfortable, painful, even intolerable. It can create feelings of tension, frustration, and even anger. When we are faced with something we do not like, that is uncomfortable, or painful we are motivated to reduce or eliminate it. This is how the law of uncertainty motivates people to reduce uncertainty through the process of uncertainty reduction. We reduce uncertainty to reduce tension, frustration, and discomfort.

Uncertainty reduction can help us to create predictability, stability, and security improving our quality of life. When bad things happen, we seek to understand them in order to reduce uncertainty and its impact on us.

It is our need for uncertainty reduction that has motivated most of human behavior throughout history. Much of what we have created in society has been done to improve our lives by reducing the effects that uncertainty has on us. Exploration reduces uncertainty about the world around us. Science and medicine reduces uncertainty about our bodies and the illnesses that afflict them. Agricultural and technological advances have reduced uncertainty about the things we need to survive like food and shelter.

So, why don't we know everything we need to know? We may have been created by nature, but nature didn't reveal everything to us. We could have been created with all the knowledge we need about ourselves and the world around us from the time we are born.

We could live in a world that we know everything about, inhabit bodies we fully understand, or have the ability to know what will happen in the future. If we lived in a world where there was no uncertainty, we would not have to solve many of the problems we face. But that was not the case, it was not what nature intended. If everything was created for a reason, then nature had its reasons.

Uncertainty motivates our behavior by forcing us to communicate with one another. It motivates us to take action to do everything that people have done since the beginning of civilization. If we had all the answers, we wouldn't have to look for them. Instead, we are forced to find them for ourselves leading to the creation of society as we know it today. Virtually everything that people have done since the beginning of time has been motivated by their need to reduce uncertainty in order to fulfill needs and wants.

By being unable to fulfill all our needs and wants, we are not always certain how they will be fulfilled. This creates uncertainty that can make us uncomfortable motivating us to take action. We want to know how our needs and wants will be fulfilled. We like stability and predictability because it is comfortable. In order to reduce uncertainty we have learned to communicate with one another, we have learned how to find out more about the world around us, and we have learned how to better understand ourselves.

From the moment we are born, as well as from the beginning of human history, people have been motivated by uncertainty to learn about themselves and the world around them, so that they could fulfill their needs and wants.

When we do not know about something we need or want, we are motivated to create new knowledge through research, exploration, discovery, invention, or creation. We are motivated to learn and develop skills giving us a sense of purpose and fostering personal growth. If we knew everything, we would not be as motivated to do these things. We would be deprived of the sense of wonder and amazement at the creations that surround us. We would not fulfill important needs like our need for accomplishment, to feel useful, to contribute, to help others, for self improvement, and to find our own sense of purpose. It would inhibit development of our self-concept and who we are as an individual.

So, what if there was no uncertainty? If all of our needs and wants were fulfilled and there was no uncertainty we would probably just sit around not doing much of anything. Without uncertainty we would not have the same motivation to communicate and work together with one another. This would make it less likely for people to have accomplished everything that has been accomplished throughout human history.

Without uncertainty we would all likely have the same knowledge reducing individual differences. There would be no need to seek out new knowledge, facilitate change, and do the things that make our lives better. If we knew everything we would not be motivated to do the things that makes society work and we would miss out on some of the most important and rewarding aspects of life.

People often ask, why doesn't God answer our prayers? Since God knows everything, why hasn't he told us more? We pray for answers, but don't always get them. Think about what would happen if God gave us all the answers. What if your children knew how to do everything for themselves? Chances are they would think they didn't need you and not ask for your help. We want our children to need us, to ask for our help and advice.

If God told us everything we wanted to know and bad things didn't happen to us, there would be little uncertainty, so there would be little motivation for us to ask for help. Society and human advancement as we know it would probably grind to a halt because no one would have any need to do much of anything. By facing uncertainty and adversity, we are motivated to find ways to solve our problems for ourselves by communicating and working with others.

The origin of the law of uncertainty.

If uncertainty was created by nature, then where did it come from? Where did it first originate? Just as physicists look for the origin of the universe, what was the origin of human behavior? What started the chain reaction that has shaped human behavior throughout history? The origins can be found in a story that we all know.

The origin of uncertainty can be found in the Bible, Torah, and Koran. All three chronicle a similar story about how God created the heavens, the earth, and everything contained within. Then God created the first man and placed him in a garden that was full of food to eat and a river with water to drink. God saw that man was alone and needed companionship, so he created woman. All their needs were provided for so there was no uncertainty.

Then God made one condition, instructing them that they were not to eat the fruit of the tree of knowledge of good and evil. Since God has knowledge of everything, he must have known what was going to happen. Did God give man the free will to make a choice that would affect all humanity, so that man would take the responsibility for what God knew had to be done?

With all their needs and wants fulfilled, God needed to motivate them to do what must be done to create society, but couldn't make them leave because they had been given free will. They had all their needs and wants fulfilled, but they wanted more. They had needs and wants they were willing to take a risk to fulfill, like gaining new knowledge.

When they ate the fruit of the tree their eyes were opened to good and evil. So, God cast them out of the garden for disobeying him. This constitutes the first account of a big bang type event in human behavior that introduced absolute uncertainty into the world because they no longer had stability, security, and predictability. They no longer had all their needs fulfilled. Now they had to provide for themselves.

When they ate of the tree their eyes were opened and they saw clearly. They shared meaning about themselves and their surroundings. They made garments for themselves and were sent out to farm the land where they would have children. Now they had to invest in relationships with one another. From now on they would have to fulfill their own needs and wants. This event set off a chain reaction that has been the catalyst for human behavior and how we have communicated with one another ever since.

Other cultures and religions throughout history have told a similar story about the origin of uncertainty. Greek mythology tells the story of Pandora, the first woman on earth who was created by Zeus, the ruler of the Greek gods. She was given a vessel and instructed not to open it for any reason. Overcome by curiosity, she opened it and all the evils of mankind were released into the world.

The world would now experience work, hardship, sickness, and the other evils of life creating absolute uncertainty. Whether we believe in these stories or not, there was a point early in history when humans appeared on this planet having to fulfill their needs and wants creating uncertainty.

Since the earliest times in history, the law of uncertainty has motivated human behavior. We all have needs that must be fulfilled in order to survive, however, there is uncertainty about how they will be fulfilled. This led to the pursuit of uncertainty reduction, which has dominated most of human behavior throughout history.

At one time people were hunter gatherers roaming the countryside looking for game to hunt and food to harvest in order to fulfill their need to eat for survival. They fulfilled this need by hunting and gathering food, which led to a nomadic lifestyle moving to wherever food could be found. They didn't always know for certain what they would find and if they did not find any food, they would probably go hungry. This way of life contained a high degree of uncertainty.

Motivated by the need to eat and the uncertainty of hunting and gathering, people took action to develop agricultural alternatives like farming and ranching. By growing their own crops and raising livestock, people fulfilled their need to eat by reducing uncertainty creating stability and predictability.

No longer needing to move from place to place, they could now fulfill their needs by staying in one place for long periods of time. They were now able to invest their time and other resources in one place creating communities. So, uncertainty reduction to fulfill our basic needs led to the creation of many important institutions fundamental to developing society, making people's lives better by giving them security and stability.

As people developed the agricultural means to reduce uncertainty, they had more time to spend on other things. Since we were created not knowing everything about ourselves and the world around us, this time could be channeled into fulfilling other needs and wants like the need for knowledge by making discoveries about the world around them, creating inventions to help make life easier, for self expression through the arts, and in many other areas that helped to develop society.

People could have been satisfied with what they had, however, as needs were fulfilled wants became needs and people developed new wants. The difference between perceived needs and wants and our expectations of their fulfillment creates uncertainty that motivates us to find ways to fulfill them.

Since people have virtually unlimited wants, when some needs and wants are fulfilled, they develop additional ones they seek to fulfill. This need to find something new and better motivates exploration, creation, innovation, and discovery. This is how uncertainty can motivate people to improve their quality of life.

People need change and excitement, they want new and better things. They have a need for more, to have more things and better things. This need motivated them to develop trade with other people in order to reduce the uncertainty of obtaining what they want. As society developed, new things became available.

Imagine what it was like hundreds of years ago to experience eating corn, potatoes, or chocolate for the very first time having never seen them before. Instead of having to find what you need or want, the establishment of trade provided a more stable and secure means of getting things people wanted.

Reducing uncertainty by fulfilling needs and wants led to increased communicating between diverse peoples and cultures. In doing so, they shared stories about themselves, their experiences, their traditions, and their history. They exchanged local foods and different ways of doing things. Through trade, not only were goods exchanged, but also ideas that benefited society.

We want to know what to expect from others in order to reduce uncertainty so that we can trust them. However, if we do not know what to expect, it will increase our feelings of uncertainty about them. The level of uncertainty we feel about other people can change because people do things that make us feel more or less comfortable with them. The degree of uncertainty we feel about others is often based on how closely our perception of them fulfills our expectations of them.

While uncertainty originates in nature, it is people who determine what to do about it. When we experience uncertainty we compare our perceptions to our expectations. If there is a noticeable difference between them, it can either diminish or intensify our feelings of uncertainty. People receive information that increases their apprehension and perception of uncertainty motivating them to take action to reduce it.

This can take intangible perceptions of uncertainty and create tangible consequences. For example, economic uncertainty can motivate people to cut spending even though they may not need to, which decreases economic activity creating a self perpetuating reality of its own.

Uncertainty can be helpful.

While we spend much time and energy to reduce uncertainty, having a manageable level of uncertainty is preferable to completely eliminating it because having some uncertainty serves important functions for us as individuals and for society. For example, uncertainty is created because we all know that we will get old, may become ill, and eventually die. This uncertainty has motivated us to develop our faith, religion, and sense of morality including our notion of right and wrong, without which the world would be a very different place.

Uncertainty is important because it can open our mind to new ideas. It makes us question our assumptions to ascertain their validity. It motivates us to adapt and rethink what we already know. It motivates us to look at what we know in new ways to come up with something better than we had before. It encourages us to change and try something new. And it motivates us to take action.

However, we do not have to wait for difficulties caused by uncertainty to motivate us to look for new ideas and try new things. We can choose to open our mind and think about alternatives before we are forced to do so. While uncertainty may not always happen in positive ways, it does motivate us to look beyond what we already know. This is how we gain new knowledge and make it useful to us.

So, why don't some things work out? When things work out for us the tension uncertainty creates is resolved. We feel more comfortable so there's less motivation to do something and we don't think as much about it. Our mind moves on to more pressing matters. If things don't work out, we need to think about them in order to work things through and look for alternative solutions.

When something doesn't work, it represents an unresolved state that creates tension making us uncomfortable motivating us to take action. It increases uncertainty motivating us to go beyond what we already know to gain new information and try new ways of doing things to resolve it. We have lots of things we need to do, so we have to prioritize what to do first and the more something makes us uncomfortable, the higher priority it gets. If everything worked out for us, we would be less likely to challenge ourselves, gain new knowledge, or open our mind to new possibilities.

Change is uncomfortable because it takes time and energy. Since we don't know what might happen, it can create more uncertainty. So, in order for us to change, the current situation must become uncomfortable enough to overcome the discomfort it takes to change. When we are aware of how this process works, we do not have to let uncertainty frustrate us, we can use it to our advantage. We can be open to new information and ideas to initiate change in our own time and on our own terms rather than being forced to change by circumstances. Uncertainty can be ironic, when we fail to take the initiative to do these things ourselves life can have a way of making us do it.

While reducing uncertainty can generally be a good thing, too much uncertainty reduction may not be good. When we are sure about what we are doing and feel like we have everything figured out, we are not looking for new information or new ideas. In this frame of mind we can be less open to the possibilities that may be available to us.

When we feel we have set goals, objectives, or a plan of action we may not consider that there may be better alternatives. This state of mind can create reduced awareness of the situation, which limits our possibilities and options. When we think we know what to do, we have less motivation to look at other options. When we are less aware of what is around us we might pass up opportunities by pursuing a steadfast single path.

When we reduce uncertainty it increases our confidence motivating us to take action. The danger is that when people feel reduced uncertainty, they may not be open to new information, so it can close them off from considering other ideas or alternative ways of doing things. It can cause them to filter out information and not listen to others who may have something to contribute. It can cause them to discount or filter out information that may be helpful. In extreme cases it can turn into arrogance creating an attitude that "I know what I'm doing." This can create the conditions that lead to bad decisions with potentially disastrous consequences.

This can happen when we are overly certain or when we think that we know what to do, so we do not stop and consider alternatives that might provide better choices. When we are certain, we are less likely to question our assumptions and the quality of our information. When we are certain, we do not look for flaws in our reasoning or test the validity of our solutions.

When we are certain, we are in the frame of mind to get things done the way that we want, rather than considering the ideas of others. When we are certain, we know that we are right and do not stop to think that we might be wrong. When we are certain, we do not need to learn anything because we know what we are doing. When we are certain, we do not look at different ideas and people who have them are viewed as disruptive troublemakers.

Extreme certainty is not the same as knowledge, expertise, experience, or confidence. Knowledge gives us information we can use. Expertise can provide us information and skills to handle uncertainty. Experience hones those skills in actual situations. And confidence gives us a belief in ourselves and our abilities.

We can have all these things while still utilizing uncertainty to bring in new ideas in order to innovate and facilitate change. If everything was created for a reason, then uncertainty was created by nature for a reason, to provide us a means to motivate change and innovation. Having an awareness of how the law of uncertainty works helps us to avoid pitfalls, so we can use it to our advantage.

Uncertainty and the stop sign.

To illustrate how uncertainty affects our behavior think about what we do when we are driving and see a stop sign or stoplight. We have to see the sign, understand what it means, and then act accordingly. The sign does not stop our car, so why do we really stop?

We stop because of the law of uncertainty. Because there's a chance we might get hit by another vehicle or be pulled over and given a ticket that would cost us time and money. We stop because it reduces uncertainty by giving us reasonable expectations of getting safely across the road.

Uncertainty can create stability by keeping people within the limits of acceptable behavior. By not knowing with certainty the future results of our actions, we are more likely to be more careful and less risky in our behavior because there is a fear of potential negative consequences.

The law of uncertainty motivates our behavior by keeping us within the rules of social reality and society. It inhibits us from taking too much risk or engaging in overly dangerous behavior. It motivates us to question ourselves and our actions, which is necessary in order to find the best solution and course of action.

All of our lives contain some degree of uncertainty. In order to reduce it, it is helpful to understand how it affects us in our own lives. What makes the difference is what we do about it. It is through increased awareness of how uncertainty works and how it acts in our lives that gives us the options that will help us to reduce uncertainty and its negative effects, while utilizing positive ones. One thing about life that is certain, there will always be uncertainty.

Shared Meaning

The law of shared meaning is the second law of behavioral communicating. It is like the law of uncertainty in that it is created by nature, not by people. It is like the law of gravity because it affects everyone whether we want it to or not. It cannot be changed or eliminated. It affects how we communicate and share information with one another. It gives information significance to help make it useful to us. It helps us to understand and make sense of our experiences. It helps us to understand ourselves and develop our self-concept.

When something contains meaning it helps us access additional information from our experiences that may be useful, so we don't have to get all the information we need every time we do something.

We are motivated by the law of uncertainty to create and share meaning, so that we can understand others to work with them and form relationships. This helps us to make sense out of our experiences to help explain what has happened in the past and better understand what we can reasonably expect in the future. Sharing meaning helps develop feelings of stability and security because we have a better understanding of others and the world around us.

Our life consists of a series of experiences, some of which may not make sense motivating us to wonder why they happen and what we should do about them. In order to reduce the uncertainty that would be created if these were perceived of as just random events, we want to understand them better by looking for meaning in them. In order to do this, we may share our experiences with others to get their insight about what happened to us and they may share their experiences with us in return.

Sharing our experiences with others creates a mutual understanding, which gives us a deeper meaning reducing uncertainty that can help make similar situations more understandable in the future. Shared meaning provides us a way to communicate with one another so we can share information about ourselves.

Much of how our identity is created is through our experiences and sharing meaning about them. How we communicate our experiences helps develop our own sense of self-concept and identity. When we share our experiences with others they learn about who we are and we learn about them, which can help to reduce uncertainty so that we can develop relationships with them.

We all have needs and wants that necessitate help from others to fulfill and the law of shared meaning helps us to understand others so we can do this. It helps us to agree on the nature of what has to be done and how it is to be accomplished.

In order to work together, we have to understand each other to know what things mean. Sharing meaning helps us to fulfill mutual needs such as safety, security, and stability, which in turn reduces uncertainty.

Throughout much of human history people have sought to know more about what was happening in the world around them. This motivated them to understand things like the changing of the seasons, how to grow crops, why they got sick, and their relationship with God. They looked for information to explain these things based on what was available to them at the time.

Throughout history as people encountered uncertainty they looked for ways to understand what they experienced. Early Greek and Roman cultures sought to explain what they experienced by creating mythology. Later, people looked to religions and sacred texts.

More recently people utilized science and empirical research methods to understand their experiences. These approaches helped them to create and share meaning to better understand themselves, others, and the world around them.

When people share stories with one another about their experiences it gives them deeper meaning. When these stories are shared they form a bond between people creating a common culture. Often these stories have a deeper meaning sharing important information.

Telling stories has become a part of society because by sharing experiences, people not only communicate information they share emotions, attitudes, values, beliefs, and a part of themselves. By sharing stories people communicate who they are, their history, and their aspirations which helps to reduce uncertainty and create trust enabling them to form relationships.

Shared meaning is often communicated in the form of stories told about people, events, and our own experiences. We tend to alter what really happened by editing events to emphasize some things, leave some things out, or add embellishments to others. This gives them a sense of drama to make them more exciting. We do this to make them more interesting to cut through the interference, so people will listen to us.

The law of shared meaning affects how we interpret our observations, thoughts, feelings, and experiences to make sense of them. It shapes our view of practically everything. In order for us to reduce uncertainty, we need to know more about others, ourselves, and the things around us. We all have thoughts, feelings, and ideas, however, others cannot hear what we are thinking, so we need a way to share that information with them.

We can get information for ourselves, but that takes time and energy. This motivates us to seek it out from others, so we need a means to communicate information in a way that is useful to us. In order to do this, we need a shared understanding of what things mean.

This need motivated people to develop a common language as a means of sharing information by utilizing symbols which are invested with meaning. By giving symbols like letters and words meaning, we can communicate with others to share information in a way that we all understand.

However, this is not the only way we share meaning. We also utilize nonverbal information by investing practically everything around us with meaning. In order to reduce uncertainty about ourselves, others, and the world around us to help us fulfill our needs and wants, we need a means to share information by communicating. This is how the law of uncertainty creates the law of shared meaning.

How the law of shared meaning works.

You have likely experienced something that illustrates how the law of shared meaning works. Have you ever attended a party, wedding, or other event with a friend who knew everyone there, but you didn't know anyone? They probably talked, laughed, and shared stories about mutual friends and experiences with one another. If you didn't know anyone there you probably felt awkward, out of place, maybe even wanted to leave.

What you observed is how the law of shared meaning works. The others were able to take what they communicated and add additional information increasing its meaning and significance making it more useful to them, while you probably didn't know what they were talking about. What you experienced is what things could be like if there was no shared meaning.

The law of shared meaning can be illustrated by how we interpret information. To demonstrate how this works, find a book that has pictures of people you know and another book that has pictures of people you don't know, along with their names and some kind of other information about them like a school yearbook.

Look at pictures of people you don't know. You can see what they look like, read their names, and understand the information about them. You probably won't have much additional information about who they are other than what is printed in the book. Now look at the book with pictures of people you know. Read their names and the information about them. You might recall things about them, things they did, perhaps even feelings or emotions. What you are thinking and feeling contains information that is beyond what is printed in the book.

When we see people we know, we recall things about them like the things that they did, perhaps even feelings or emotions. You might have feelings of warmth and affection or perhaps dislike or agitation. You might remember things you did together that makes you laugh. What you are thinking and feeling contains information that is beyond what is happening in the present. It's like a connection is made and something opens up. It's a very different experience than when we see or talk to people we don't know.

If there were no law of shared meaning, what we communicate to others would be more like looking at pictures of people we don't know. We could communicate with one another, but there would be little additional information available making it more difficult to understand them. We would have to explain practically everything every time we communicated.

Having shared meaning gives us a reserve of information that we can call up without having to communicate it or have it explained to us every time we needed it. Shared meaning is how we make sense of the world around us. It is how we interpret our observations, thoughts, feelings, and experiences. It shapes our view of practically everything because it influences how we see ourselves, others, and the world around us.

The origin of the law of shared meaning.

The origin of the law of shared meaning can be found in the same places as uncertainty. God created the first man and saw that he was alone and needed companionship. So, God created woman and provided for all their needs. God instructed them not to eat the fruit of the tree of knowledge of good and evil.

When they did eat from the tree, their eyes were opened and they both saw clearly and they knew good and evil. They now shared new meaning about themselves, each other, and the world around them originating the law of shared meaning. Then, they were cast out of the garden and no longer had all their needs provided for, so now they had to provide for themselves.

Since our needs and wants motivate us to take action by communicating with others, sharing meaning helps us determine what things mean and what actions to take. The meanings we share can determine our behavior. For example, we share meaning about things like the weather.

At one time, people found meaning in the lack of rain and the failure of their crops to grow as God's displeasure with them or they made sacrifices to their gods. Today, when there's a lack of rain and failure of crops we interpret it as weather patterns brought by the jet stream and build irrigation systems. This means that the same set of circumstances, influenced by different shared meanings, motivates distinctly different behavior.

When we communicate with others we look for shared meaning not only in what they say, but also in what they do. We tend to interpret what people do, how they look, their facial expressions, and many other nonverbal elements by giving them meaning. Meaning is found not just in the words people say, but also in how they say them. We even find meaning in what people do not say. We look for meaning in these things so we can understand others better to reduce our uncertainty about them.

The nature of shared meaning.

Shared meaning gives us a sense of our identity as an individual and as a member of groups. Through the process of shared meaning when we communicate with others they respond with feedback that affects our perception of who we are. We share different meanings with others based upon the nature of our relationship with them such as our friends, family, or coworkers. We get a broader perspective about our experiences when we share them with others. When many people share their experiences, it creates a common history that develops culture. It is through shared meaning that we come to understand our relationships with other people.

We share meaning about what other people say and do in order to reduce uncertainty and to make them more familiar. When people are unfamiliar, we do not know what they might do and so we might be less willing to communicate or work with them. However, we need others to help us fulfill our needs and wants which motivates us to find meaning in what they do.

So, we gather information by observing what people say and do. In order for that information to be useful, we interpret it by giving it meaning. Often we don't have enough information so we make inferences to fill in what's missing. This gives us an idea of what a person is like so that we know what we can reasonably expect from them to reduce uncertainty.

The law of shared meaning enables us to share knowledge so that we can learn from the experiences of others. As we all have things that we need to know and learn, we can gain information from others without having to figure everything out for ourselves. New information can be added to what people already know, growing the body of knowledge.

Many of the things we need or want to do have already been done by someone else, so we can benefit from their knowledge and experience through the process of shared meaning. We can take what is meaningful to others and make it useful to us without needing to have the same experiences. Without the law of shared meaning, developing and sharing knowledge would be more difficult.

The law of shared meaning makes possible many things that are essential to everyday life. Perhaps the most important is how it enables us to communicate with each other through a common language.

Developing language is the process by which people create symbols, like letters and words, and invest them with meaning. Sharing meaning enables us to communicate with one another using a language that everyone understands. By giving symbols meaning, we can more easily and effectively communicate information and store it for future use.

Language often communicates other information about a person when they speak such as their culture, ethnicity, education, vocation, and how they view the world. Having a common language not only permits people to communicate and understand one another, it also creates a common bond giving them a sense of mutual identity that brings them closer together.

The shared meanings that are in language reduce uncertainty because if everyone gave different meanings to the same things, we would not understand one another. Understanding is necessary for society to function and it occurs when we share meanings. When it doesn't, it can lead to misunderstandings, tension, conflict, and even hostilities.

We invest meaning in people we don't know as well as people we know like our family, friends, coworkers, or neighbors. We give meaning to our past experiences in order to add significance to our lives. We give meaning to the things that we enjoy such as art, literature, and music.

We give meaning to geographic locations such as where we were born or where we live. We give meaning to our culture, ethnicity, nationality, and religion. Practically everything we do, everyone we know, and everything around us we invest with meaning and we share these meanings by communicating with others.

Traditions and rituals like holidays, celebrations, birthdays, anniversaries, and other occasions when people get together are an important way that we share meaning. We celebrate these events because of their significance and participate in them to share their meaning through our actions.

Sharing traditions and rituals gives us a sense of who we are, where we have come from in the past, and our expectations for the future. It makes us feel closer to others and part of a group with whom we share the same experiences. It connects us to the past and our ancestors, as well as to future generations. This helps make us feel a part of something greater than ourselves, which reduces uncertainty about ourselves and others giving us a feeling of stability and security.

The law of shared meaning makes society possible. By sharing meanings we communicate what our country stands for and what it means to be a citizen. We communicate our collective history and traditions, values and beliefs. This creates a set of shared meanings that can be easily understood by members of a society as well as by outsiders.

These meanings shape the perception people have of a country and its citizens as well as who they are and what they stand for. It creates a sense of collective identity as people see themselves as a citizen of a country. How members of a nation or society share meaning can be a powerful force because it has the ability to motivate their attitudes and actions on a large scale.

The law of shared meaning leads to investing because when people give things meaning they also give them value. Giving something meaning gives it significance and significance increases its importance making it more valuable.

This is because when something is important to us we are willing to do more or spend more to obtain it or keep it. We place value on people in relationships, on things and possessions, on intangible concepts such as skills or knowledge, and on practically everything we find around us. Value is often based on comparisons gained from our perceptions to create expectations. We use our perception based on currently available information and compare it to our expectations for the future. This can motivate us to rank things by their importance, which can help us to set priorities.

We often value things based on how useful they are to us in fulfilling our needs and wants. We place more value on relationships that fulfill important needs and wants. Shared meaning can determine what things we value based on our feelings about them. We place value on things that we feel an emotional attachment to or that are part of our past experiences. Other times we value something based on what others think about it.

Through the process of shared meaning, if people value something others are more likely to place a value on it. By sharing meaning we come to know how important, valuable, and useful things are. In this way sharing meaning has tangible and monetary consequences.

Investing

The law of investing is the third law of behavioral communicating. It is similar to the laws of uncertainty and shared meaning because it was created by nature, so it cannot be changed by people. It is like the law of gravity because it affects everyone whether we want it to or not. It was formed by the other two laws in order to make them work.

We can reduce uncertainty and share meaning, but we need to take action for anything to happen. In order to reduce uncertainty and share meaning, we must invest our time and other resources in ourselves and others.

People may react to the first two laws by simply hunkering down and living in a cabin in the woods. However, the law of investing forces them out into the marketplace of human activity. The law of investing regulates how we manage our resources and negotiate with others for our mutual benefit to fulfill needs and wants, so we can accomplish our desired outcomes.

This creates a kind of behavioral communicative marketplace where people make and receive offers utilizing their resources to obtain their desired outcomes. Communicating is the currency of this marketplace because it enables us to invest these resources. This is the fundamental process that makes human behavior work by connecting us to others.

We all have needs and wants that we cannot fulfill ourselves, so we need help from others to fulfill them. Other people also have their own needs and wants that they cannot fulfill themselves, so they also need help. This puts everyone in the position of wanting things, but needing help from others to obtain them.

Having our needs and wants fulfilled often comes at a cost. We have resources of value that others need and they have resources we want. The most familiar resource is monetary, but we more often utilize other resources like our time, attention, effort, energy, expertise, experience, and skills. When we have unfulfilled needs and wants it can be uncomfortable motivating us to communicate with others, so we can invest in relationships to achieve our mutual desired outcomes.

When this process goes smoothly everyone can benefit, however, there are times when it does not. People can have virtually unlimited needs and wants to fulfill with limited resources. We often have conflicting needs and wants. We may feel we are contributing to others, but not receiving what we need in return. This can create tension and even conflict, which can force us to make choices about our relationships and how we communicate with others.

For example, if we do not feel we are being fairly paid for the work we are doing, we might want to quit our job. If we feel we have been contributing to a relationship where the other person is only taking and our needs are not being met, we might want to breakup. This is how the law of investing can exert powerful forces that motivate our behavior, the decisions we make, and how we communicate with others.

In order to invest in others we need to reduce uncertainty. When we feel a great deal of uncertainty, we are reluctant to invest our resources because we do not know what to expect in return. When we reduce uncertainty, we are more likely to invest making us feel safe and secure because we have reasonable expectations about what we will receive in the future. The less uncertainty we feel, the more comfortable we are sharing our resources in order to help others fulfill their needs and wants. This also makes it more likely for them to help us fulfill ours.

Not only do we seek to reduce uncertainty to invest, but we also invest to reduce uncertainty. We invest our resources in relationships and activities that will benefit us now and in the future. For example, we invest time and energy in a job to receive not only a salary, but also for the safety and security that comes with it. This can help us to fulfill other needs like buying a house, having a family, or retirement.

The law of shared meaning helps us to invest because it increases our mutual understanding of one another. When we share meaning with others, we feel we get to know them better so we know what to expect of them in the future. This can increase stability and security making us feel more comfortable investing our resources. The more we feel safe and secure, the more we are likely to invest ourselves and our resources in relationships without expecting an immediate return. This helps create the long term stability necessary for creating and maintaining meaningful relationships.

The origin of the law of investing.

The origin of the law of investing can be found in the same texts as the laws of uncertainty and shared meaning. When God created the first man and placed him in a garden, God saw that man was alone and needed companionship and so created woman. Then God instructed them not to eat the fruit of the tree of knowledge of good and evil. When they ate the fruit of the tree God cast them out of the garden. Now Adam and Eve no longer had all their needs provided for, so they had to provide for themselves.

They no longer had stability, security, and predictability. After Adam and Eve left the garden they had children. From now on all people would be different because they would not be created directly by God, as were Adam and Eve, instead they would be created by people through reproduction.

This meant that from then on people would be responsible for the creation of life, so they would have to invest their time, energy, and other resources in relationships including families, groups, and communities.

Nature created people with the ability to self-replicate by having children for the continuation of humanity. However, nature provided only one method of human reproduction to create new life. From the moment they are born, a child is totally dependent on their parents and will need their family to fulfill their needs and wants for many years to come. Because of how we were created, we must invest in relationships with others not just for survival, but also for our well being.

Nature could have created us different. We could have been created to have children as a single individual or by another process of reproduction as happens with other forms of life. We could have been created by nature to be more self-reliant when we are born. We could have had the ability to care for ourselves sooner or to mature faster as do other living things.

But that was not what nature intended. Nature intended for us to need other people. Our needs motivate us to create and maintain relationships with others like our family. These relationships help us to fulfill our needs and wants making the law of investing a powerful force in our lives.

The marketplace of communicating.

When we communicate with others we often make verbal and nonverbal offers that are either accepted or rejected. This process works rather like the trading floor of a stock market. This happens in our daily activities, so it goes mostly unnoticed.

This marketplace is driven by how we communicate with each other, so communicating could be characterized as its currency. In order to fulfill needs and wants, people enter the marketplace and negotiate with others by offering resources and seeking investments in return. It is through communicating that we negotiate what we are willing to do and what we might expect in return.

This negotiation may be overt and out in the open or it may be covert like when we try to cover up our intentions. We may be aware of what we are doing or we may do it by habit. Whatever the case, we are generally aware that we are doing something for someone else so they will do something for us. This negotiation is sometimes expressed when we say things like, "I owe you one."

People invest to reduce uncertainty, but how much they are willing to invest depends on their individual needs and wants, how much they think others have to contribute, and what they are likely to receive. Our perception can be affected by how well, or not so well, similar investments have gone in the past. This can motivate us to invest more in some relationships and less in others.

The level of investment is not only a matter of how much people are willing to invest, but also how long they are willing to wait before receiving a return. Sometimes we do very little to get what we need. Most impersonal relationships don't involve a great level of investment, like when we ask for help from a store clerk.

Then there are more personal relationships that require long term investments like a spouse or family. The level of our investment can have less to do with our satisfaction with a relationship than it does with our perception of what needs and wants we have fulfilled.

We make many low level investments without even thinking much about them. For example, we might help a friend carry their groceries or a coworker fix a printer. Most things we do are low level investments, so we do them without thinking much about them. However, they do provide an indirect reward because doing them is the right thing to do. When we do the right thing, it shows that we are a good person so we feel good about ourselves.

Medium level investments are the things we do for others without asking for much in return. However, most of the time we expect to receive some benefit. It could be saying thank you or the expectation of them reciprocating in the future. For example, if we help a friend move or drive someone to the airport, there is the expectation that they would do the same for us in return.

If a person does not reciprocate, we may become put off or offended even though we did not originally ask for anything. Even if we do not expect something in return for our investment, doing something selfless can give us a positive feeling and bolster our self-concept, which is in effect a positive reward.

Then there are high level investments that we make in relationships with others such as our family or job. These are relationships in which we invest a great deal of time and energy with the expectation of receiving benefits that fulfill important needs and wants. Many times we are glad to do things because we feel we are contributing and making a difference without directly expecting a return.

We make investments in our family because we are expected to do this and that's what families do. What we receive in return is fulfillment of many of our most fundamental needs and wants such as safety, security, stability, affection, or intimacy.

At work we have the reasonable expectation of receiving a salary and other benefits. We are often willing to put in our time and other resources now with the expectation of future rewards such as a raise in pay or a promotion.

Uncertainty and economic equilibrium.

Many times we evaluate the success or failure of our investments based on our perception of the return on those investments. For example, if we have a job where we feel we are working long hours and spending a lot of time and energy, we may feel that we are not getting the recognition we deserve or are not being treated fairly. This perception could make us upset and even angry to the point that we ask for a raise and if we don't get it, we might quit.

If we have a job where we feel we are working reasonable hours with reasonable demands, and are paid well for what we do, we likely feel valued and happy with our job. We certainly would not want to quit. This is one way that the law of investing can affect our state of mind motivating our actions.

Communicating can be an indicator of value. People tend to communicate about things that are important to them, so you can determine what they value by measuring the amount of time and effort they spend communicating about something. We tend to not communicate about things that are not very important to us or things in which we have no interest. In order to connect with others and have them understand you, it's helpful to know what they value. This can be measured by the amount of time they spend communicating about it.

By listening to others, we can know what is of value to them and determine what would make them more likely to invest. Since negotiation takes place through communicating, it's possible to analyze what is going on in any communicating marketplace by measuring its activity. This works rather like stock prices or economic indicators that can be used to explain what has happened in the past to provide some indication of what might happen in the future.

Conventional approaches suggest that in a marketplace people seek to minimize costs and maximize rewards, in other words they buy low and sell high. However, when it comes to communicating with others, this is not generally the case. It may be more the exception than the rule because most people do not behave in this manner.

This is because when one person seems to be benefiting much more than others, it creates an imbalance that can damage relationships. They may be seen as being self-centered and others may feel that they are not being treated fairly. No one wants to feel that they are being treated unfairly by being around a person who contributes as little as possible while seeking to gain as much as possible by buying low and selling high.

Everyone does not seek to maximize rewards, instead they are more likely to look for rewards to fulfill their specific needs and wants. They look for balance by receiving a fair return based on fair investments. In this approach, a person may be the most satisfied by being slightly ahead, breaking even, or even having a small loss. This makes the break even point or achieving economic equilibrium an important factor in determining relational satisfaction and if they feel like they are being treated fairly.

Not everyone follows typical patterns when it comes to needs and wants fulfillment. Some people behave contrary to the conventional wisdom of investing to fulfill needs and wants. They may forgo their own safety and material comfort to live in rough conditions so they can help others. They may give up lucrative careers to pursue endeavors they enjoy that pays very little.

While this behavior does not follow the convention of buy low sell high, it follows the laws of uncertainty and investing because people invest in order to fulfill their individual needs and wants, which helps to reduce their feelings of uncertainty.

However, under the law of investing, they are maximizing their investment based on their perception of what fulfills their needs and wants. This is because our needs and wants are more than just monetary, they can be spiritual, being needed by others, making a difference, feeling appreciated, or doing the right thing. When people want monetary rewards, what they may really need is recognition or status. For most people the rewards that are the most important to them are generally not material or monetary.

The law of investing can affect how happy we feel. All too often we find ourselves in relationships that aren't working and then wonder what's wrong. How we balance costs and rewards in relationships can be an indicator of several things. In order to better understand what these things are, you can create a balance sheet by listing your needs and wants in order of importance.

For each one, ask yourself how well are each of them being met? When they are being reasonably met, it can make us feel good. When they are not being met, we can feel unhappy, even frustrated. When we understand how the law of investing works, we can use it to restore economic equilibrium by balancing rewards and costs.

We are more likely to be satisfied and feel good about a relationship when we feel we are making fair investments and receiving fair rewards. When we feel that others are contributing to the relationship we are more likely to be committed and contribute to the relationship as well.

The Rules of Communicating

The laws of uncertainty, shared meaning, and investing were created by nature to motivate human behavior. In order for people to effectively utilize these laws, they developed rules for behavioral communicating. Rules govern human behavior by letting people know what is expected of them in just about every aspect of life.

Rules tell people how to reduce uncertainty, they regulate how people share meaning, and they let people know what they can expect when investing in themselves and others. Rules are often developed by people over long periods of time. While they can be changed, this can be slow or difficult to do.

Rules help us to fulfill our needs and wants, so we generally agree to abide by them because if we did not life would be much more chaotic and it would be almost impossible to function. Rules allow the marketplace of communicating to function properly, so people can create relationships in order to fulfill their needs and wants.

Nearly all human activities, groups, and organizations have their own set of rules which have been developed to meet people's needs and wants by regulating their behavior. Rules are necessary in order to reduce uncertainty, so that people know what is expected of them and what they can expect from others enabling them to work with one another.

A good example of why rules were created and how they work is illustrated by those used in sports. Many of the sports that we are familiar with today, like basketball or football, at one time did not exist. They were created by people who got together to fulfill mutual needs and wants like having fun, to compete, or to be part of a team.

In order for them to do this they had to create rules that governed their behavior, so that everyone knew what to expect. The rules changed over time to meet the changing needs of the sport and its participants. Without rules no one would know what to do and everything would breakdown into chaos.

Rules of society work much like the rules of sports. They were created by people so that they could function together in a mutual activity to fulfill their needs and wants. For rules to work everyone must agree to abide by them. They regulate behavior so people know what to do and what to expect.

Rules tend to change slowly over time to accommodate changing circumstances while maintaining stability. They are mutually beneficial because without rules no one would know what was going on and there would be chaos.

Rules facilitate the process of shared meaning to reduce uncertainty, which encourages investing in others, groups, and in activities. They enable us to communicate more effectively with one another, which helps us to fulfill our needs and wants.

It can be helpful to clearly communicate the rules because they create stability to reduce uncertainty by letting people know what is expected of them and what they can reasonably expect of others. Otherwise, they may try to circumvent rules they see as not in their own interest or that prevents them from getting what they want.

The Process of Communicating

The process of communicating provides a way to look at how we communicate by understanding individual elements in the process. It helps us to see how these elements work together so that we can be better understood by other people. We often communicate without thinking how things work so when they don't go as we want, like when we are misunderstood, we may not know how to fix them.

By understanding the process of communicating, you can develop skills to communicate more effectively with other people. How people communicate involves a number of elements that occur seamlessly so that we don't think much about them.

Therefore, it can be helpful to describe the process to help understand how it works. How communicating works is often illustrated in a technical way using boxes, triangles, circles, arrows, and lines to connect things to other things. However, communicating is not about technical or abstract things, it is about living people who are active and dynamic. These human characteristics are reflected in the process of communicating.

You, your desired outcome, your Great Idea, others, connections, The Great Abyss, feedback, and effectiveness are all elements in the process of communicating. They provide a clear and accurate way to talk about specific parts of the process we use to communicate. Being aware of these elements and how they work provides a way to talk about how we communicate, so that we can communicate more effectively with others and improve our communicating skills.

The process of communicating consists of these elements.

1. You. You are the creator and communicator of your message, so the process of communicating begins with you. Everyone communicates for a reason because we have thoughts, ideas, and feelings we want to share with others. Since everyone is unique, you have your own unique way of doing things that includes your own style of communicating.

These characteristics are what gives you your own unique personality. Many of these attributes affect how you communicate with others and can help or hinder you getting your message across to them. Some of these are changeable and some are not. Becoming more effective at communicating involves knowing your own individual style of communicating and being able to adapt your style to the situation, while still being yourself.

Everyone has a different style of communicating. Some characteristics that influence your style of communicating include your background, interests, and experiences. A person's first interactions are with their family, so this is where they first learn how to communicate with others. People may keep these ways of communicating throughout their life. A person's experiences affects how they communicate, so if they find a way of communicating with others that works for them, they are likely to keep using it.

Everyone has a different set of communicating skills. This can affect how they communicate with others because people who have well developed skills tend to feel more confident, so they can be more likely to communicate with others especially in uncertain situations.

People who feel they do not have communicating skills tend to hold back and may not participate as fully. This can give a false impression that they are not interested or are aloof. So, it can be helpful not to judge people just on their communicating skills, but on what they have to say.

2. Desired outcome. We communicate not only to share information and to understand each other, but also to get things done. We often determine what we want in terms of achieving goals and objectives, but desired outcome is different. Goals and objectives can be specific things we want to achieve, so we develop a plan and pursue a course of action that can put us on a single path leaving little room for alternative ways to achieve them.

This can prevent us from noticing alternatives that may be preferable. There may even be the chance that the goal we are pursuing is not the best one for us. By pursuing goals and objectives we can lose out on potential opportunities that present themselves along the way.

We often characterize getting what we want as achieving a goal or objective. Using sports as an example, a goal or objective can be considered analogous to making a goal, basket, home run, or touchdown. It is a clear, definite action that is either accomplished or not.

Since not every team can win every game, goals and objectives can be discouraging. They can even hurt your self-concept and sense of well being. A desired outcome approach would focus more on a general sense of well being such as personal growth and development, working better as a team, and enjoyment of the game regardless of winning or losing. While losing a game will not accomplish your objective, you can still achieve your desired outcome.

This concept can be applied to our careers and personal lives as well. For example, you may want to advance in your job, but you don't get the promotion you feel you deserve, so you leave and move to another job. While this does not achieve your goals and objectives, the new job may be better for you by providing more opportunity in the future.

Considering your desired outcome provides a more positive result than simply achieving goals and objectives because there could be things going on that you may not be aware of, which might affect your achieving them. For instance, your old company may have had underlying problems that might have prevented you from advancing or being happy there.

While losing a job is not necessarily a good thing, it may provide time for other more important activities you would not otherwise have time to pursue. It could motivate you to improve your education and other skills, to pursue important interests, and to develop better relationships with people who are close to you. Pursuing the desired outcome of increasing your job satisfaction and financial stability can put you on a different path helping you to achieve it in the long run.

Everyone communicates for a reason and desired outcome is a part of that reason. Desired outcome is what you want to happen after others get your message. It is more general in nature and considers the big picture, which gives you more ways to achieve what you want. Desired outcome encourages you to consider multiple paths to select the most effective one and to switch them as needed or if you run into difficulties. This enables you to pursue opportunities that may present themselves along the way. Desired outcome focuses less on achieving specific goals or objectives and more on fulfilling needs and wants which provides more options to fulfill them.

While your desired outcome is about what you want to happen after you communicate with others, rather than looking for something specific to happen, take a big picture approach focusing on your general state of well being. This increases the number of ways to reach your desired outcome providing you with more flexibility.

Increased flexibility can improve your effectiveness and the likelihood that you make it happen. It can reduce competitive pressure to win by reducing the prospect of losing by not achieving your goal. If one approach doesn't work, there may be other ways to achieve your desired outcome. This helps to create a more positive climate that can encourage others to work with you to achieve your desired outcome.

When you know your desired outcome you can spend time on what really matters. Everyone has tasks to accomplish, but desired outcome is more than that. Simply accomplishing tasks themselves may not achieve our desired outcomes. This can be why we might feel that we are working all the time, but not getting anywhere. This could be one reason seemingly successful people may be frustrated, because they focus on accomplishing tasks or achieving goals and objectives, while neglecting their desired outcomes.

Focusing on achieving your desired outcome can be a more positive approach because it is less discouraging when what you want to happen does not happen. It helps us avoid making judgments about things being good and bad or feeling like a failure. It allows us to find partial success in what we do because pursuing a desired outcome considers the big picture in the long term as a general state of well being.

There are times when we try to achieve our desired outcome and things don't go the way we would like them to go. These situations could be characterized as resulting in unintended or undesired outcomes. An unintended outcome is a result that we did not expect, it can be positive or negative or a little bit of both.

We may have asked for a raise, but instead we were given a promotion or had a pay cut. One was positive and the other was negative, however, we did not intend either to occur. An undesired outcome is when we get a result we do not want. We may want to get a raise, but end up being fired. We never wanted to be fired and if given a choice would have stayed at the same salary. Because it is undesired, it is generally considered negative.

While we can never be certain what other people will do or how they might act, we can utilize our knowledge of the process of communicating and our own skills to avoid unintended or undesirable outcomes. It can help to look at your desired outcome from the point of view of the other person and to consider how they might react. All too often we concentrate on what we want to happen instead of thinking about what others might do in response. No matter how effectively we communicate, there is always the possibility that instead of achieving our desired outcome we might get an undesired or unintended outcome.

3. Your Great Idea. Your Great Idea is the information you want to share with others. It is the part of the process of communicating that begins with your message, which is what you say or write, but it can also consist of many other elements such as nonverbal information including facial expressions and gestures. It usually starts with an idea that exists in our mind not just in words, but also in pictures.

In order to communicate Your Great Idea to others, it has to be in a form that others can understand. This usually involves putting ideas into words that are spoken or written. The words and letters themselves are just symbols that have no inherent meaning. The meaning is given to the symbols by people who translate them into words in order to communicate them to others. When they receive the message, they translate the words back into ideas to understand them.

We use the law of shared meaning to go through this process of investing symbols with meaning and translating that meaning into ideas. We do this so often it happens naturally without much thought. When we speak, our mind automatically translates our ideas into words and when we read or hear words they are automatically converted into ideas. This means that the meanings are in the minds of people and not necessarily in the symbols themselves.

For example, when you see the word TREE, you don't think oh, that's four letters. In your mind you see a picture of a big green plant with a trunk, branches, and leaves or needles. This is because everyone who understands English has learned that these four letters are symbols that represent a big green thing. The word TREE is not really a tree.

Using symbols is critical to communicating because if every time we wanted to communicate the idea of a tree, we would have to describe it or show one to others and that would take a lot of time. Instead, we take the symbols T R E E and invest them with meaning so the letters become a shorthand reference that refers to the real big green thing.

4. Others. Others are the people with whom you want to communicate. In the process of communicating, everything begins with you so anyone else you communicate with whether it's just one person or a large number of people are referred to as "others." Just as you communicate with others for a reason, others listen and communicate with you for reasons of their own.

Since every person is unique, other people have their own way of doing things, which includes their own style of communicating. This can include their own individual characteristics that give them their own personality. These characteristics can affect how they communicate with you. This can help or hinder the communicating process and how well your message comes across to them.

To communicate effectively, it is helpful to know and recognize the unique communicating styles of others to help adapt your own communicating style to them, while still being you. The same things that influence your style of communicating such as family, culture, education, religion, and geographic affiliation also influence how others communicate with you.

How others communicate is based upon their background and experiences. No two people have the same experiences, even those who grew up in the same family. Even people who experience the same events have different perceptions of them.

People are more likely to communicate about things that they are interested in or things that they have strong feelings about. They are more likely to communicate about something they are interested in or that they like. Being aware of this can help you to communicate more effectively with others.

Everyone has different communicating skills. Some people are more experienced making communicating easier for them, while others may have fewer skills making it more difficult for them to communicate with others.

Awareness of their skills and how comfortable they are communicating with others can help you to communicate more effectively with them. Sometimes a perceived unwillingness to communicate with you is not about you, but rather about the other person's comfort level with their communicating skills.

In order to effectively communicate with others, it's helpful to be aware of what things might influence how and why others communicate with you. By knowing this you can avoid perceiving their lack of communicating as personal because it may be due to some other factor. No matter how much we may want to, we are unlikely to change how other people communicate and what they do.

However, we can change the way that we communicate with them. By having an awareness of how the process of communicating works and how it affects others, we can adapt our own style to communicate more effectively with them.

5. Connections. Once you have created your Great Idea you need a connection to get it to others. A connection is the means by which you connect to others so that they can hear or see your message. Creating a connection is essential to effectively communicating with others. If there is no connection, they cannot get your message. Some common connections include speaking face to face, telephone calls, writing a letter or email, public speaking, or through the public media.

We make connections with others using our five senses. When we speak or listen to someone, we make an auditory connection. We use gestures and facial expressions such as smiling to communicate nonverbally, so others see us through a visual connection.

Shaking hands or patting someone on the back makes a connection using touch. Wearing perfume or cologne or offering them food makes a connection using our sense of smell. Sharing food or drink, like dinner or coffee makes a connection utilizing taste. Most of the time making a connection involves using more than one of our five senses.

We all have different ways that we obtain and retain information. When you use multiple connections appealing to more than one sense, you increase the chance that people understand and remember your message.

For example, if you want your children to be on time for dinner, you could utilize multiple connections through different senses. You can use an auditory connection by telling them. You can use a visual connection by leaving a note on the refrigerator where they will see it. You can use smell to make a connection by having food that smells good to attract their attention.

On a romantic date we can make several connections to communicate including visually with our appearance, auditory by playing music; with the smell of cologne, perfume, or flowers; taste with food; and by touch. Increasing the number of connections can make an experience more intense.

Just as we make connections with others we also can become disconnected. We can become disconnected intentionally by no longer talking with someone such as the result of a disagreement. We can become disconnected unintentionally when a relationship drifts apart over time. It can be interrupted by interference and the things that get in the way when people are busy.

We can lose touch with coworkers when we change jobs or neighbors when we move to a new community. This can happen for no apparent reason and can leave us feeling frustrated, depressed, or a sense of loss.

By being aware of how the process of communicating works, we can make choices about how we connect or disconnect with others rather than letting it just happen and then end up wondering why it did.

6. The Great Abyss. In the process of communicating, you share your Great Idea to others by making connections with them in order to achieve your desired outcome. In an ideal situation they would receive and understand your message, however, in reality other things can get in the way. Making a connection with others does not necessarily mean that they will understand your message. The Great Abyss represents increased uncertainty and the lack of shared meaning.

Sometimes when we communicate with others, there is a huge chasm that separates you from them. In order to effectively communicate with others, you must make a connection to get your message across this chasm without it getting lost. This chasm can be characterized as "The Great Abyss."

The Great Abyss can alter how others perceive your message and even stop it from getting through to them. It can be thought of like a chasm that has to be crossed in order to make a connection with others. It characterizes everything that can potentially get in the way of you effectively communicating with others, so that they don't get your intended message.

Instead, they may get a different idea, the wrong message, or nothing at all which could result in undesired or unintended outcomes. This is why understanding what is in The Great Abyss can be helpful to effectively communicate with others.

The Great Abyss consists of interference that prevents others from understanding your Great Idea. You can interfere with your own message when it is unclear, confused, or disorganized. This can be overcome by using methods of organization, clarifying information, and seeking feedback from others to make sure they clearly understand your Great Idea. Interference cannot only create uncertainty, it can increase it.

By being aware of how interference works, you can cut through it by emphasizing key points, repeating information, seeking out feedback from others, or asking them questions. It can be helpful to cut through interference to help others better understand your message.

Internal interference includes things that occur in people's minds that interferes with how they perceive your message like a short attention span, being tired, overworked, bored, or having too much to do. They may have different backgrounds, education, experiences, or expectations.

Everyone has their own point of view based on their experiences. It influences how they communicate and affects what they pay attention to or ignore. It affects how they interpret and understand what you communicate to them.

Frames of reference work like the frame of a window or the viewfinder of a camera. It determines what a person perceives because everything outside the frame is blocked out or ignored, and they may not be aware that they are doing it.

Preconceptions block information that is contrary to people they feel they know. For instance, if they have one political point of view they may block out information from other political points of view that contradict their own. Because people tend to be more receptive to messages that fall within their preconceptions, it's helpful to know what they are, so your message fits them.

Filters block out certain messages, because we get so much information we have to filter some of it out. This is why people pay attention to what they feel is important and filter out everything else.

Interference can be illustrated by how we perceive road signs when we are driving. We do not pay attention to all the signs we pass because we see so many. If we paid attention to all of them it would hinder our driving. However, if we are almost out of gas we pay attention to every sign looking for a gas station.

So, if we need or want something we are less likely to filter it out. By knowing how this process works, we can communicate more effectively with others. By being aware of how interference works, you can cut through it by using repetition, emphasizing important points, asking questions, and getting feedback.

7. Feedback. So, you have your Great Idea, made a connection, and crossed The Great Abyss to communicate it to others. How do you know if they got your message? Utilizing feedback is the best way to find out how effectively your Great Idea has been received.

Feedback can happen in a variety of ways. It can happen informally by asking questions or having others restate your ideas to determine if they fully understand them. Feedback can happen in formal ways such as surveys, interviews, polls, or focus groups that can be used to determine the effectiveness of media messages like an advertising campaign.

It is important that feedback be accurate and honest. A face to face conversation is the best means of feedback because it is instantaneous and offers the widest variety of channels to communicate. Other types of feedback such as surveys and polls can be helpful, but can be less accurate as people may not be motivated to participate, may provide incomplete information, or give the answers they think makes them look the best.

8. Effectiveness. Effectiveness is the degree to which others receive your Great Idea and you achieve your desired outcome. We might characterize some ways of communicating as good and some as bad. For example, if someone doesn't understand us, we might think that we did a bad job of communicating with them. If we speak in front of a group and it doesn't go well, we may feel that we are not a good speaker.

Thinking about communicating in these terms does not help us improve our skills, which can be discouraging. If we feel things didn't go so well, it can increase our anxiety making us reluctant to do it again. A speech that might have been considered bad could in fact have been somewhat effective in getting your message across. By trying this approach, you can determine how to make it more effective. Rather than thinking in terms of good or bad, think of communicating effectively.

Effective communicating is the degree to which you achieve your desired outcome. The more you understand others and the more they understand you, the more effectively you can communicate with them.

Looking at how you communicate in terms of effectiveness rather than good or bad, can help you to determine what works and what could be improved. It can give you a more realistic idea of your skills so that you can feel better about what you can do and work on developing what could be done better.

Styles of Communicating

When people create their Great Idea they may use a particular style of communicating to make a connection with others. In order to communicate more effectively, it is helpful to recognize these styles and be aware of their strengths and weaknesses. How people communicate with others can be characterized by three basic styles.

The first style is the arrow approach. This style of communicating is similar to shooting an arrow into the air and hoping it hits the target. In this approach, a person creates their Great Idea, they construct a message, send it to others through a connection, and then wait for the result. They hope it hits its target and is understood. The people who receive it may not fully understand the message or may interpret it differently than it was intended.

While this sounds like an ineffective way to communicate that can easily create misunderstandings and increase uncertainty, it is how people have been communicating for a long time. Much of the news and information we receive that influences our perceptions and expectations, and shapes social reality is communicated through the media using this approach.

This method of communicating is similar to the military where a commanding officer sends a message down the chain of command to the troops in the field who are expected to follow orders. Then the commander waits for the result. At one time this style was considered successful, so it was adopted by businesses.

A CEO could be considered a kind of commanding executive officer who sends orders down the chain of command to each level of an organization telling employees what to do. This style lacks an effective means to provide feedback to know if a message was received or understood.

The second style is the tennis approach. This style of communicating resolves some of the problems with the first style. People need to know if their Great Idea is accurately received, so this approach provides a way to get feedback from those receiving the message. This encourages the people receiving the message to communicate back to the person who sent it to determine how well it was understood. The sender could then decide if additional information is necessary to clarify it.

This approach works like tennis where one person creates their Great Idea and then hits it over the net hoping the other person will get it. If the other person returns the ball it's a success. We use this style when we send emails, memos, and phone messages. This style offers some improvement over the first method because there is a mechanism to provide feedback to clarify the original message. It is commonly used even though it can be awkward and time consuming.

The third style is the conversational approach. This style fixes most of the problems of the first and second styles. It is more realistic and effective because it takes into account all aspects of the process of communicating. It works like having a conversation where people are talking to one another. They are communicating information and providing feedback simultaneously to facilitate understanding.

This is the most effective approach, however, it can take the most time and energy. It is often preferred because it takes into account the individuals involved and the context of the situation.

This style is referred to as a conversational style because it is like having a conversation where people both speak and listen as well as provide information and ask questions simultaneously. Rather than being a process of one side against the other, it provides a collaborative process for people to work together to achieve a common understanding.

This style works when instantaneous feedback is useful to help the process. For example, if you are trying to fix a computer it can be difficult reading a manual and could take forever to get the information you need using email. Having a conversation provides direct feedback to make the process quicker and easier.

We use this style when we see someone face to face and have a conversation or when we speak to them over the telephone. This is a more effective means of communicating because we get results immediately rather than waiting for feedback.

A short conversation can accomplish more than dozens of emails because we can communicate exactly what we want, clarify information, answer questions, and resolve things much more quickly. However, people may avoid it, using the other two styles by texting and emailing because they can be reviewed and edited before sending. They may feel conversation is too spontaneous or risky increasing their anxiety and uncertainty.

In order to communicate more effectively, it is helpful to recognize when to use each of these styles of communicating and why. While the third style is the most effective, consider just how often people use the first two. We tend to get in the habit of using the first two styles because they can be easier and quicker. They save us time and allow us to make a connection, while still keeping a distance. Each of these styles can be useful depending on your desired outcome, but they also have their limitations.

Chapter 2
The Nature of Reality

Everything created by people has one thing in common, at one time it did not exist. It first existed as an idea in a person's mind who then, following the process of communicating, had to make a connection to communicate their Great Idea to others who had to understand it for it to become reality.

This process of developing ideas and communicating them to others works not only for tangible things people create, but also for concepts and ideas. Often these ideas shape how people think and motivates their behavior creating physical reality. When people use this process to communicate their ideas to others, it helps to create social reality.

When we think of reality, we think of things like tangible objects that actually exist as opposed to something intangible that exists in our mind. We don't necessarily consider concepts that exist in our mind as reality.

However, communicating the thoughts and ideas that exist in our mind can become as much a reality as the tangible things all around us. What we think about and communicate to others can create a reality of its own.

Consider the following types of reality.
1. Physical reality.
2. Social reality.
3. Group reality.
4. Individual reality.

1. Physical reality.

Everything around us can be divided into two basic categories, everything created by nature and everything created by people. Everything created by nature is governed by the laws of nature, like the laws of physics. Physical reality includes everything that exists in nature such as all living things and naturally occurring phenomena.

Some physical reality is created by people including tangible material objects like houses, clothing, and furniture. When we invest physical reality with meaning motivated by the law of shared meaning we create social reality.

However, people don't only deal with the physical world, they must communicate with one another to fulfill their needs and wants. So, people create social reality because it is more familiar reducing uncertainty.

2. Social reality.

Social reality is how we make sense of physical reality. It is created by people through the process of communicating with one another. People are motivated to create social reality by the law of uncertainty in order to reduce uncertainty. Social reality reduces uncertainty because it provides the information, structure, and rules people need to function in society.

Social reality shares meaning because it comes from people's experiences and interactions. It allows investing because it creates stability so people know what to expect. It can be seen as an organized collection of rules, shared meaning, and the common expectations we have of ourselves and others.

Social reality can create physical reality. While social reality primarily exists in our minds, it can become as real as physical reality because of its power to motivate people's behavior. Social reality is how we interpret the information we gather creating our perspective of how we see ourselves, others, and the world around us.

Often the events that happen to us and the things we see around us are open to different interpretations. Social reality tells us which interpretations are acceptable and which ones are not. It can determine how we react to events and what we do about them. It influences how we interpret our experiences and the experiences of others.

Social reality manifests itself in tangible objects that we create. This can change over time affecting our physical reality. Even though people's needs have remained much the same throughout history, how they fulfilled them has changed considerably. For instance, we need to wear clothes, but the way we dress is determined by what social reality tells us is acceptable. It once motivated women to wear corsets and men to wear tights.

Social reality can determine what ideas are considered acceptable and how they should be implemented. This can be illustrated by how people have interpreted the nature of government. Throughout history, people have formed governments motivated by similar needs for security and stability, but have created very different physical realities.

In ancient times, rulers claimed they were descended from the gods or ruled by divine right. Later, monarchs were chosen by birthright. More recently, elected leaders are chosen through democratic means by the will of the people. Different social realities based on different cultures and time periods manifested themselves in different physical realities.

Social reality is attractive because it answers many of the most fundamental questions about life for us. We don't have to figure everything out for ourselves if we choose not to do so. Instead, we do what social reality tells us to do. We do this because figuring everything out for ourselves takes time and energy, so there is an advantage to invest in a particular social reality.

We might try to work things out for ourselves, however, we run the risk of being perceived as being wrong. So, we go along with others because we feel they are knowledgeable and the details are taken care of for us, so we don't have to work everything out for ourselves.

Social reality can be analogous to having your taxes done. Everybody has to do their taxes and if you don't there are penalties. To do this we have two choices, to do it ourselves or to have somebody do it for us. Doing it ourselves takes time and energy, but we have a better understanding of what we did and may have learned something in the process.

Having somebody else do it is easier because they fill in all the blanks and all we have to do is sign on. However, we may not understand everything we are signing. The same could be said of social reality. We join groups and organizations so someone else will fill in all the blanks to answer some of life's important questions. All we have to do is join and go along because we may increase uncertainty if we try to come up with the answers on our own.

Social reality is created by people to reduce uncertainty found in physical reality, so they can better understand and find meaning in the things that they perceive around them. It fulfills several needs including our need to create order out of chaos, our need to organize things around us, and our need for control. It tells us how we should act and what to do in various situations. It influences our behavior and keeps us in line with what is considered acceptable.

These are all important functions for society because they reduce uncertainty and create stability. We know what is expected of us and what we can expect from others. However, it has the potential to give enormous power to those who create it.

Social reality gives us the ability to create and share meaning. We use it to interpret and invest physical reality with meaning. It helps us to take the unfamiliar and make it familiar. It takes chaotic events and makes them understandable by giving them meaning so they can be useful to us.

Social reality is an important mechanism we utilize to deal with the unpredictable and chaotic events of life. We create and share social reality so we can invest in ourselves, others, and society.

Social reality works because it fulfills many of our most fundamental needs including our need to know more about ourselves, others, and the world around us. It fulfills our need to exert control over a chaotic world by explaining how it works. It exerts social control over people to create a stable society.

Social reality enhances our understanding of things around us because it fills in the gaps in our knowledge and understanding. We cannot possibly experience everything, so we rely on social reality to fill in what we do not know.

The power of social reality is in its ability to motivate behavior by altering how we interpret our physical reality. For example, at times people have interpreted the lack of rain that made for a poor harvest as God's displeasure with them. Some cultures responded to this physical reality with human sacrifices, others sacrificed animals, and others felt they needed to atone for their sins by praying more.

Today, we explain the lack of rain as being due to weather patterns, so we develop drought tolerant crops and build irrigation systems. In each of these societies, differing social realities explain the same physical reality in different ways motivating people to take different actions. This makes social reality very powerful, even potentially dangerous because it motivates what people do about what they perceive.

Social reality can be a form of social control because it motivates and shapes our behavior by telling us what is socially acceptable and unacceptable, including what we can and cannot say or do. So, it not only serves to motivate our behavior, it may constrain it as well. In this way it can limit our choices exerting influence over us. People make choices and decide how to act based on the rules and expectations of social reality.

While this sounds restrictive, and it can be, without social reality everyone would behave differently and no one would know what to do or what to expect from others. People behave differently enough as it is, imagine what life would be like without having social reality to regulate behavior. This would add to the level of uncertainty making life even more uncertain.

Social reality helps to bring our intangible thoughts and ideas into existence in physical reality. Everything created by people existed first in someone's mind who, through the process of communicating, shared it with others. As more people shared the idea it became a part of social reality.

Even though social reality exists primarily in people's minds, it manifests itself in their behavior, actions, and how they communicate with others. Through their actions, it can create its own reality that can be as real as physical reality.

3. Group social reality.

Groups and individuals can create their own specialized version of social reality by adding their own ideas to meet their specific needs, wants, and desired outcomes. Group social reality often includes stories about how the group began, its founder, well known members, its history, significant events, and what it means to be a member.

Social reality can develop slowly through people sharing meaning over time or be created intentionally in a comparatively short period of time. Some types of groups that develop their own specialized social reality include educational, religious, political, military, and cultural groups. Tension between differing social realities can be a source of conflict, even violence or war.

A group social reality is often created to fulfill the needs and wants of the group. It can be used to encourage commitment to the group. It may be communicated to the public in order to gain outside support or recruit new members. For most of these groups their shared group reality fits in with the larger social reality. Artificial social realities can be developed by groups like political parties in order to promote a specific political agenda or to support candidates for public office.

Religion is an example of how social reality reduces uncertainty, shares meaning between people, and encourages them to invest in themselves and others. All religions serve a similar function and have similar elements, but these can be manifested in distinctly different ways. They answer some of life's most perplexing questions like who we are, why we are here, and where we are going.

Religion interprets events and invests them with meaning. They have a history, traditions, and rituals that create and maintain connections between people. Their power is in how they take ideas and manifest them in physical reality, motivating the behavior of large numbers of people. How they accomplish these things is often contingent on their place of origin and the time period in history when they were established.

4. Individual reality.

An individual social reality is how we as an individual organize and make sense of the world. Not everyone subscribes to every aspect of the larger societal social reality, nor do they have to in order to function in society. However, this flexibility can manifest itself in differences that can create tension and even conflict between people and within society. These differences enable us to create our own individual reality that can fall within the larger social reality, but can also deviate from it in certain aspects.

We may subscribe to part of it, but then alter or change other parts to fit our personal needs and wants. We do this because it helps us get through everyday life. Without it things would be more difficult. Since we created it, we can change it when it suits us.

However, like our self-concept, an individual reality develops slowly over time, so that we may not even be aware of it. Our individual reality includes how we see ourselves, others, and the world around us. Awareness of this type of reality is important because of the influence it has on how we communicate and how it motivates our behavior.

At times different social realities can compete and even come in conflict with one another. This is because they may be based on different cultures, countries, religions, or political social realities that may not be compatible. Some people may belong to different groups that have conflicting social realities that can create confusion or tension. To resolve this tension we could develop our own version that combines elements from several other social realities.

Social Reality and Dramatic Narratives

When people communicate, they talk about themselves often telling stories about their past experiences. When they do, they might edit these stories to make them more interesting and exciting to others. When people understand and can relate to these stories, they share meaning. They have the same understanding of what they mean and possibly share their own stories about similar experiences. This can create a connection, so they feel that they have something in common. This can make people seem more likable, even creating feelings of empathy.

The process of sharing meaning deals with the human tendency to want to understand the motivation for people's behavior to reduce uncertainty about them. Shared meaning is how a person makes a connection with other people, so that they see things in a similar way.

Shared meaning can help to recall familiar stories for those who share them. If a specific story has not been shared, it would not make sense and the entire story would have to be explained. People often create stories about themselves and their experiences to share meaning with others. They do this to make themselves more personable so people support them.

Social reality is how people make sense of the world around them. Life can be chaotic, things can happen for no apparent reason and social reality is how we organize and make sense of these things that happen to us. Social reality is important to us because it determines how we interpret our perceptions and what we do about them creating tangible consequences.

A specialized version of social reality is usually comprised of selected portions of the larger societal social reality because it has to be compatible with it in order to be accepted by the public to gain support. If not, they may be perceived as too extreme or out of touch. Then, they must make a connection with the people and communicate their message to them so that they will understand it. This is commonly done through the use of dramatic narratives.

It could be said that forms of communicating fall into two categories, fact and fiction. There is the inherent assumption that if a person is not telling the truth they are lying. So, if fact comprises those things that are verifiably true and fiction is an imaginative creation that does not represent actual reality, people who share meaning through dramatic narratives utilize neither fact nor fiction. Instead, they take an inherent reality, like the economy or health care, select a few pertinent items, and present a dramatic narrative that is their characterization interpreted to fit into their version of social reality. This maneuvering between fact and fiction falls within the realm of dramatic narratives.

In dramatic narratives events are explained to create and sustain shared meaning with other people and to support a specific version of social reality. Much of our social reality is constructed through dramatic narratives. They are often given a dramatic, persuasive, or emotional quality to make them more interesting or dramatic. This helps to cut through the interference of the Great Abyss, so that people will pay attention to them.

Dramatic narratives often include heroes and villains, along with characterizations of their actions as being good or bad. A person might cast themselves in their own dramatic narratives as the hero who will save the people from a villain who is out to destroy everything they hold dear. These dramatic narratives are often action based in order to involve the people who must take action, along with the hero, to save them from a terrible fate if nothing is done.

Over time, many dramatic narratives can form a recognizable and meaningful view of society that helps to create social reality. The power of social reality lies in its ability to explain our experiences and the world around us reducing uncertainty. The sharing of social reality is a way of creating a common understanding of the world and how it works.

The shared meaning contained in dramatic narratives can create a social reality for people. Even though it may or may not accurately reflect actual physical reality, it may be no less real for them. The creation of social reality is motivated by people's need to reduce uncertainty by explaining events in order to make sense of them.

Social reality is created because people want to reduce uncertainty. They want to know about the world around them and social reality can be used to explain and predict physical reality. For instance, people want to know why the economy is bad and when things will get better.

They want to know what they can expect from their government and what the government expects from them. These issues are often explained through social reality. This means that social reality can be as important to society as physical reality because much of human interaction and public institutions are socially constructed.

Social reality can be powerful because it tells people how to interpret physical reality and what to do about it. It can be used to explain events by telling people what is happening to them and how they fit in. It can be used to explain the motivation for people's behavior. It tells them what behaviors are accepted and which ones are not. It can serve as a comprehensive explanation of how things work in society. It can also facilitate confidence in societal institutions by reducing uncertainty about them. People often prefer a reality of their own making, one they have created themselves because it is more comfortable when it is made up of familiar elements.

Changing social reality.

While the larger social reality must change, once we adopt a particular social reality it may be difficult to change because it provides us with stability and security. We might react negatively to others who try to change it because change represents increased uncertainty. This is because social reality becomes a part of who we are and our self-concept, so we may see attempts to change it as threatening.

We may resist change because if one part of what we believe is wrong, other things we believe could potentially be wrong as well. This can make us feel uncomfortable because it could undermine our feelings of safety and security increasing uncertainty. This motivates people to defend their version of social reality even when they suspect it's no longer accurate.

Change is inevitable and unavoidable. If social reality never changed we would still think the Earth was flat and the Sun revolved around the Earth. In the past, people have resolved the tension created by conflicting social realities through various means including violence, war, and revolution. For example, the American Revolutionary War was about more than independence from England, it was to legitimize the changing social reality about self determination in government.

Having the ability to create a mechanism that allows social reality to adapt and change is essential to growth. Maintaining a constant social reality may be comfortable, however, without change to reflect changing needs and wants it would be nearly impossible for us to function in a constantly changing world. This may be one reason why young people can be more adaptable to some things than older people because their individual social reality has not yet been fully developed for as long a period of time. It has likely undergone change more recently, so change is more familiar creating less uncertainty.

While social reality governs how society works, in order for society to develop it needs a mechanism that allows for change while maintaining stability. One way this happens is through creative expression. Some groups and individuals such as artists, writers, fashion designers, actors, and musicians differentiate from accepted social reality by creating a specialized individual or group reality.

This allows new ideas like artistic tastes and fashion trends to be tested and accepted before they become part of the larger social reality. For instance, there was a time when rock music and impressionistic painting were considered scandalous, but today they are considered part of our culture. This mechanism allows for new shared meaning to be created without excessively increasing uncertainty.

The Perception Process

Perception is how we gather information and give it meaning, so that it can be useful to us. We gather information through our five senses: sight, sound, taste, touch, and smell. We also gather information through other means such as our feelings, emotions, intuition, and impressions. Perception is much more than just receiving information, it is about what we do with this information. Perception is the means by which we get to know what we know. It is how we make sense of the world and influences how we communicate with others. Everything we know and think including how we view ourselves and others is created through perception.

Perception is important because it is not only the process by which we gather information, it is the process by which we come to understand it. It is how we make sense of ourselves, others, and the world around us. It is through perception that we create personal and social reality. It is how we learn by observing and doing to create new knowledge. Perception gives meaning to our experiences. It provides us with the information we use to solve problems and make decisions. It is how we develop our attitudes, formulate our beliefs, and establish our values.

By understanding how the perception process works, we can become more aware of our choices and have more control over how we utilize the information we receive. The perception process may provide information, but the information we receive can affect how we perceive things.

When people get information that is not current, accurate, valid, or is biased it can create perceptions that are not accurate. This can result in unrealistic expectations altering their view of social reality. We perceive information all the time without thinking much about it, however, effectively utilizing it takes effort. Having an awareness of how the perception process works enables us to take control of the information we perceive rather than letting it control our thoughts and actions.

The perception process is motivated by the law of uncertainty. It is through our perceptions that we gain information and knowledge to reduce uncertainty about ourselves, others, and the world around us. This is how we share meaning with others. It's how we gather, organize, and give information meaning so that it is useful to us now and in the future. We use our perceptions to determine whether or not to invest our resources in others and in relationships. The perception process provides the information we need to make decisions and solve problems.

Interference can hinder our perceptions blocking out potentially important information. Our filters and frames of reference determine what information we actually perceive. Our perception is affected by the filters we use to remove information we don't consider useful and frames of reference that help form our point of view. By being aware of the perception process and how it works, we can improve our own process of communicating to communicate more effectively with others to reduce uncertainty.

Everyone has their own point of view that makes them perceive things differently. This is why several people can see the exact same event, yet they can give distinctly different accounts of what happened. The individual nature of the perception process can make eyewitness testimony one of the most unreliable forms of evidence.

This occurs because perception is a complex process of selecting, interpreting, and organizing the information we perceive through our five senses. Often there is more information than we need, so we select what is important or interesting to us and discard the rest.

How we make sense of what is around us is based upon the choices we make about how we use this information. Because it is important how we act around others, it helps to understand how the process of perception, selection, organization, and interpretation influences our behavior and how we communicate with others.

1. Selection. Selection is about what information we choose to perceive. We make choices about what information is important to us and what is not. There is often more information available to us than we can utilize, so we must select what we feel is useful and filter out the rest. Selection is making choices about what information to keep and what to discard. It's a natural process so we generally don't think much about it.

We select information based upon our personal preferences, experiences, and what we feel will fulfill our needs and wants. We are more likely to pay attention to information that is about things we like or that we find interesting. We have a tendency to look for and select information that fits in with what we already know because it fulfills our expectations reducing uncertainty. When we feel we know and understand things, we feel more confident and better about ourselves.

We tend to filter out or discard information that is unfamiliar or contradicts what we already know because it can be uncomfortable. If it is unexpected, it might not fall within our frame of reference. If it doesn't fit in with our current perceptions, we are likely to filter it out.

This is a naturally occurring process because new information can create tension with what we already know which increases uncertainty and reduces stability. We tend to ignore it because if we are wrong about one thing, we may be wrong about others, which can undermine our social reality. This is why we may filter out information we might need.

Much of the perception process happens instinctively and subconsciously, however, there are times when we make conscious choices. We can choose to filter out information by withdrawing or not listening to others. We can choose to avoid unwanted information by excluding people, things, and situations we may find uncomfortable.

We make choices communicate with some people, but not others. We make choices about what to watch on television, listen to on the radio, and what to read in newspapers or look at on the internet. We select what information to allow in and what to block out. Even if we listen to someone, we may not be mentally engaged by thinking about something else that blocks them out.

2. Organization. After we select information to perceive, we have to organize it so it can be useful to us. Organization is how we arrange, sort, categorize, and fit together the information that we perceive. Information rarely comes in a clearly organized way, so we need to arrange it in a way that's meaningful to us. How information is organized directly affects its meaning and how we utilize it. We do this because when information is organized it reduces uncertainty and we can give it meaning. This makes it easier to recall making it useful to us in the future.

Much of the information we receive comes in bits and pieces. The perception process has to put these pieces of information together, so that we can better understand them. How we choose to organize information determines how things fit together rather like a puzzle.

However, this process doesn't always go easily and the puzzle may be missing pieces, so we have to fill in the gaps of missing information in order for them to make sense. Sometimes we only have fragments that do not seem to fit, so we need to find a way to utilize them. This can make us look for information so we can complete the picture. We may fill in the gaps by using inferences and other information that may not be true or accurate.

We utilize organizational methods to arrange information to make it easier for us to understand and remember. We can use methods like appearance, proximity, or similarity. We might create our own methods to categorize information by labeling things based upon our past experiences. When we come across something new we tend to organize it based upon our existing categories. If something doesn't fit into our categories, we are more likely to discard it. This is because grouping information together makes it easier for us to organize and recall it later.

Information comes to us in a steady stream often without a clear beginning or end. In order to make sense of it we have to cut it up into understandable pieces like punctuation does for words in forming sentences. A page of words without punctuation is difficult to understand because we don't know where ideas begin or end. Adding punctuation groups words together in order to give them meaning. We do the same with the information we perceive by grouping it together to give it meaning.

The perception process works a bit like books in a library. The books are organized by topics making it easy for us to find and use them. There is an established method to how they are organized so that new books can be added whenever they come in and we can find the one we want, whenever we want.

If the books were not organized this way and instead were put on the shelves in the chronological order they arrived at the library, like how we experience things in life, it would make finding the one we wanted almost impossible. This is why we may need time to process new information, so we can organize our experiences to make them easier to understand and retrieve them when we need them.

If we cannot find a place for new books, they are more likely to be discarded. So, if new information doesn't fit in with what we already know, we are more likely to reject it. By having an awareness of this process, we can develop an effective way to bring in new information without discarding what we already know.

3. Interpretation. The law of shared meaning motivates us to interpret the information we receive by investing it with meaning, so that it can be useful to us now and in the future. When we interpret information we can make comparisons between the new information and the information we already have. This helps us to determine the validity of the information and its usefulness.

This process happens primarily subconsciously, however, there are times when we become aware of it such as when something doesn't seem right. Interpretation is very subjective because it is based upon an individual's experiences, point of view, and personal social reality. Understanding how we interpret information is essential to understanding how we communicate.

Interpretation of information is important because it has the potential to not only change our perception, but our individual social reality as well. This can affect how we communicate with others, our behavior, and how we see ourselves. Generally, our perceptions do not suddenly or significantly change our social reality because we need consistency.

Consistency increases stability and reduces uncertainty, which makes us better able to function. However, there must be a way to change and adapt our perceptions in order to utilize new information. This creates tension between what we know and what we may need to know or what we perceive, which can lead to internal conflict.

How we interpret information we perceive is influenced by many factors including our culture, ethnicity, family, education, age, gender, values, attitudes, beliefs, geographic affiliation, and past experiences. It is also influenced by our needs and wants, likes and dislikes, and the perceptions we have already interpreted. The factors that influence our interpretations are important because we make judgments that affect us based upon these interpretations. They also affect what information we use to create or change our own personal social reality.

Interpretation of new information can take time and energy. This is why when something unexpected, shocking, or traumatic happens to us we may need some time to come to terms with it. We need time to process the new experience or information because it may not easily fit in with our past experiences or what we already know. This can be difficult when it challenges what we already know, our values, or our beliefs. Knowing how this process works can help us understand why we may have feelings like frustration or anger, so we can better deal with them. It is helpful at these times to allow yourself the time to process information or experiences to deal with them as well as possible.

Our mood or emotional state can affect how receptive we are to new information as well as how we interpret it. We have a tendency to be more perceptive when we are experiencing uncertainty because it motivates us to look for something new or different to improve our circumstances.

When uncertainty is reduced, we tend to be more content or satisfied with our situation and less likely to look for something new as there is less motivation to change. Alternately, people who are overly dissatisfied such as being upset or angry might reject new information because they are not able to handle it at the time.

Perception causes us to form impressions of people. Since everyone communicates for a reason, we infer that there are motives behind a person's behavior and what they communicate. When we meet someone we have limited information about them. The perception process compares what we observe to our past experiences and then we fill in the gaps to form an impression of others.

This first impression may or may not be accurate, but it can be difficult to change because we have a tendency to categorize people and experiences by grouping them together based on similar characteristics and our past experiences. We do this because it enables us to fit new information in with what we already know. This gives us an idea of what to expect in the future by reducing uncertainty, so we are more comfortable getting to know them.

Expectations

Since no one can accurately predict the future, we create expectations in order to reduce uncertainty because it can give us an idea of what the future might be like. We have expectations about ourselves, others, and practically everything around us. Without expectations, life would be more uncertain and we could not function in daily life because they allow us to do things without having to think about them.

We communicate with others in order to achieve desired outcomes, which are based on our expectations. Expectations consist of something that we reasonably believe will happen or a mental image of what something will be like. We are motivated to develop expectations by the law of uncertainty in order to have a reasonable idea of what things will be like in the future. Expectations reduce uncertainty by providing a measure of how well we are doing. If our perception of reality matches or exceeds expectation, we feel good about things. If they do not, it can make us feel frustrated, upset, or even angry.

Expectations fulfill the law of shared meaning because they give things additional meaning. Without having expectations, it would be nearly impossible to make investments in ourselves and others for the future.

Expectations make the law of investing work because without having reasonable expectations of getting a return, we would be reluctant to invest our time and energy in anything. This means that expectations often represent benefits we would like to receive in the future.

Expectations may be realistic or unrealistic, accurate or off base, but we could not function without them. When we do something for others, we cannot be sure what they will actually do in return. Without reasonable expectations of some type of reciprocation or benefits, people would not be as willing to invest their time, energy, money, and other resources in the things that are important for society to function.

We have expectations about practically all aspects of our life including what we do, what others do, our family, our friends, our job, our coworkers, and what life should be like. We have expectations not only about extraordinary events that may happen in the future, but also about everyday life. We have lots of small expectations without which we could not function.

We could not communicate with others without expectations. There are many things that we need to do to get through everyday life that would not be possible without expectations. We don't think much about them because most of the time the smaller ones are fulfilled. However, when our expectations are not realized, it can be a source of dissatisfaction, tension, and even conflict.

We need to have expectations in order to get through daily life because if we had to stop and think about each thing, it would take an inordinate amount of time and we would not get very much done. The vast majority of the time everything goes well, so we become accustomed to having these expectations met.

We get so accustomed to this that when they do not go as we expect, it can throw us making us feel frustrated or angry. The smaller the expectation, the more we might expect it to happen. This can be one reason why people blow up over small, seemingly insignificant things.

We obey the rules of society because we have the expectation of receiving rewards that fulfill our needs and wants if we do. If we did not have these expectations, we would be less likely to accept the rules of social reality and focus on fulfilling our own needs and wants first.

Instead, we may delay gratification for ourselves and contribute to others without expecting to receive something in return. This promotes acceptance in others by having reasonable expectations of future benefits.

Our feelings of satisfaction or dissatisfaction can have a lot to do with the gap between our perception of reality and our expectations. Whether we feel successful or not can be affected by the difference between our expectations of need and want fulfillment and our perception of what we have received. For example, when our perception of reality exceeds our expectations we are likely to feel happy, even elated at our accomplishments.

Conversely, when our perception of reality is below our expectations, we can feel upset, unhappy, or even angry. In each case the gap between our perceptions and expectations creates tangible feelings and emotions that can affect our behavior and actions. Our behavior can be markedly different depending upon if we feel successful or not based upon our perceptions and expectations.

Everyone's perception of reality is different and so are their expectations. A person with a seemingly high degree of success might be dissatisfied based upon the gap between their perceptions and expectations.

This may be one reason why people who seem very successful, wealthy, or famous can be unhappy, dissatisfied, even suicidal. It may be because their perception of reality does not meet their expectations. Conversely, people who may not be considered as successful can be happier, because their perceptions meet their expectations.

We all want to improve our quality of life. We have expectations that things should get better over time. If our perceptions don't meet our expectations, it can be frustrating or debilitating. It can even make us quit trying altogether. If our perceptions exceed our expectations, we may feel that everything is fine and may not do anything to improve ourselves.

In order to facilitate improvement, it can be helpful to have expectations that are slightly above current perceptions to help motivate sustained improvement. When expectations are slightly above perceptions they can seem more achievable.

If our expectations are too big it can become discouraging and if they are too small there won't be much improvement. So, in order to use perceptions and expectations to motivate behavior, set your expectations just enough above your perceptions to motivate you to improve without being discouraging.

What expectations do you have about yourself, your family, your job, your co-workers, or your life? It can be helpful to think about your perceptions and expectations. You might write them down and how well you feel they are being fulfilled. Ask yourself if your expectations are realistic or not. Ask yourself if your perceptions are accurate or not.

Tension, unhappiness, and even conflict can come from inaccurate perceptions and unrealistic expectations. By understanding your perceptions and expectations, you can determine how accurate they are and if they are a source of unnecessary unhappiness. Sometimes clarifying perceptions and expectations can make them more realistic improving your outlook on life.

We all have expectations and make judgments based on our perceptions. It's a natural part of how we reduce uncertainty. We do this so often they become second nature, so we don't think much about them until they become a problem. By being aware of our expectations, we can be more realistic about what we expect of ourselves and others.

It can be helpful to talk about our perceptions and expectations, so that we know what others expect of us and they know what we expect of them. Sometimes we feel that others just know this or will just get it. The reality is most of the time other people don't just get it, creating unnecessary tension. By communicating our expectations, we can better understand of how expectations can be managed to improve our relationships.

Awareness and options are two skills that are helpful to effectively communicate with others. Awareness is about how we gather information through the perception process, and how we use that information gives us options. Awareness is much like communicating, it is something we all do naturally without thinking much about it.

However, awareness involves developing our perception process so that we notice more of what is around us. This helps us to control how we interpret and organize the information we perceive. It is the ability to look at what you know and use it in new ways.

Awareness includes self-awareness, which is knowing our own style of communicating including how our perceptions and expectations influence our behavior. It is understanding how well our needs and wants are being met. It is understanding how others communicate, their communicating style, their perceptions and expectations, their needs and wants, and what we can do to communicate more effectively with them.

Increasing awareness can provide us with options and having options helps us communicate more effectively. Having options is not just about more choices, but having the ability to find the best one in a given situation. It helps us to not fall into the habit of doing the same things over and over when they may not be effective. It helps us to evaluate our ways of doing things to see what can be improved to be more effective.

Increasing awareness of your options can help you to achieve your desired outcomes. Awareness helps us to look at what works and why it works. Having options makes it possible for you to change or add new ideas and skills, so you can choose what works best for you.

Chapter 3
Individual Communicating

Individual communicating is about you. It is the first level of interaction because it is about how we communicate with ourselves. Our self-concept is in part developed based on how we communicate with ourselves and the kinds of messages we send. We send ourselves so many messages we may not be aware of what we are telling ourselves.

This is why it can be helpful to increase our awareness of the messages we send ourselves, so we can be in control of them in order to improve our self-concept. Individual communicating skills are important because how we communicate with ourselves can affect how we communicate with others.

So, why do we communicate with ourselves? Doing this helps us to organize our thoughts and sort out the information we receive. We do it to reduce uncertainty and learn more about ourselves, to help understand our experiences by giving them meaning, and to invest in ourselves.

This is how we process information to make it useful. It helps us to make good decisions by weighing our options and thinking things through. Communicating with ourselves helps us to increase our awareness of things that we feel are important, to work out problems, to remind us of things we need to do, or remember things we have done well. All these help us to reduce uncertainty in our minds.

Sharing meaning is essential to understanding others as well as ourselves. Much of what we communicate carries meanings that we intend as well as some we do not. Developing individual communicating skills helps us to understand not only what we mean when we communicate, but also how others perceive us.

It also helps us to better understand what others mean. Utilizing the law of shared meaning to develop our individual communicating skills helps us to communicate more effectively to create a common understanding with others.

The law of investing motivates us to invest time and resources in others. However, we also need to invest time and resources in ourselves. All too often we neglect our own needs and wants by putting ourselves last behind everyone else. Developing individual communicating skills can help us to invest in ourselves and in our abilities by improving how we communicate with others.

We have many needs and wants that we cannot fulfill ourselves. So, we need to communicate with others in order to fulfill them. Individual communicating skills can help us to communicate our needs and wants more effectively to achieve our desired outcomes. We can develop our individual communicating skills, like musicians develop skills in order to perform for an audience.

We communicate with others based upon the information that we have gathered through the perception process. We determine what information to select and how to organize and interpret it. This means that we can have the same experiences as others, but interpret them differently. By developing individual communicating skills, we can better understand the process of how we select, organize, and interpret the information we receive.

Our perceptions can create expectations. We often develop expectations by what we tell ourselves we should be doing, should be communicating, and should be receiving. For example, you may tell yourself that you should have better relationships, better pay, or more time for yourself. Eventually, you may begin to believe these expectations and act based upon them whether they are accurate or not. So, our perceptions and expectations can be based upon the messages we send ourselves, which can in turn influence our behavior.

Social reality is constructed when people communicate with one another. The messages they send create shared meaning based upon their perception of themselves and the world around them. We develop our own individual social reality based upon the messages people send us and the messages we send to ourselves.

Self-Concept

Communicating with ourselves helps to give us a sense of who we are. We are motivated to do so by the law of uncertainty because we might feel uncertainty about ourselves. When we feel that we do not know what we would like to know about ourselves, it gives us a desire to find out more. We want to reduce uncertainty about ourselves so that we are more able to fulfill our needs and wants, meet our expectations, and have satisfying relationships with others. This question gets at the core of who we are as a person and what it means to be human.

Developing your self-concept is about getting to know yourself, which can be one of the great adventures in life. We are born with little self awareness or self-concept, so we develop it as we get older. People often take time to find themselves or to get to know themselves better. We do this because of the uncertainty we may feel about ourselves, about who we are, about our abilities, and about our future.

If we had a total understanding of ourselves there would be little motivation for self discovery, personal growth, or self improvement, which would make life less interesting. A lack of understanding motivates us to know more about ourselves by looking for meaning in ourselves and in our experiences. When we understand ourselves better, we are perceived by others as being more confident and stable making them more willing to invest in relationships with us.

When we are born we know little about ourselves including why we are here. This creates uncertainty motivating us to look for meaning in our experiences to create a sense of purpose or reason for being here. One of our most basic needs is to have a sense of purpose in our lives by understanding why we were put on this Earth. By knowing ourselves better, we can learn more about our purpose in life.

How self-concept is created.

Our self-concept is the picture that we have of ourselves in our mind consisting of our perceptions and expectations. It develops slowly over time and as we get older becomes more stable and resistant to change. It is an important part of our own individual social reality motivating our behavior.

We develop a self-concept because it fulfills our need to be a unique individual. We use it to fulfill the need for prestige, respect, status, and self-esteem. It helps us to answer the question of who we are by reducing uncertainty about ourselves. It motivates us to communicate with others to gain knowledge about ourselves.

We develop our self-concept partially based on the process of reflective communicating. This happens when we create our Great Idea and communicate it to others through connections across The Great Abyss and they communicate back to us. We use this feedback like a mirror to determine how we are being perceived by others because we cannot see ourselves as they see us.

While reflective feedback has the potential to influence our self-concept, by being aware of how it works we can decide how we want to use it. We can determine what is useful to us and what is not. We can let others know if their perception does not fit how we see ourselves. When people provide reflective feedback they may consciously or subconsciously wait to see if we accept it or not. If we accept it, it may confirm how they perceive us. If we reject it or correct their perception, they may be open to changing their perception of us.

While we really shouldn't care what other people think about us, the reality is that we do. We care because if people like us then we must be a good person because people like other people who are good. Instead of using reflective feedback, we could develop a more accurate self-concept through more effective self-awareness.

We could utilize objective criteria based upon the things that we do. However, that would be more difficult and time consuming. So we use feedback from other people because it's easy to do and it happens so naturally we often don't notice it.

There are things in life that give us energy and make us feel rejuvenated. These include doing things that we like to do, being places we like to be, and being around people we like. However, we may feel full of energy and then for no apparent reason feel drained. This is because there are things that drain our energy making us feel tired and frustrated.

There are people who give us energy and those that take it from us. Because we are busy, we may not be aware of this. We may have these feelings, but do not know why. It can be helpful to increase our awareness by writing down those things that both give and take energy from us. This can provide options on how we could maximize those things that give us energy and reduce those that take it.

Self-concept and expectations.

Our self-concept can also be affected by how well our expectations match our perceptions based upon feedback from others. Perceptions and expectations are intangible qualities that exist in our mind that can create physical reality. They can influence how we communicate with ourselves affecting our behavior. Our perceptions can differ from actual reality creating an inaccurate, even distorted view of ourselves. Part of our self-concept can be based upon the difference between our perceptions and expectations because we all have expectations about ourselves and how we want others to perceive us.

If the feedback we receive meets or exceeds our expectations it can create a positive self-concept, feelings of self worth, and increased confidence. If the feedback does not meet our expectations we may become frustrated, upset, and even angry. This can be influenced in part by our perception of reality being significantly different from the actual reality that others perceive.

We may have unrealistically high or low expectations of ourselves, and when we do not receive the feedback we expect, we can have a distorted perception of ourselves. If we did not get the feedback we expect or think we deserve we may become frustrated, angry, or lash out at others.

Perception of our self-concept can be self perpetuating because we communicate with others based upon how we see ourselves. This can affect our behavior and how we communicate with them. Others perceive this behavior and may interpret it similar to how we perceive ourselves. They respond appropriately based upon their perception and interpretation of our behavior. Then the response we receive can verify our perception of ourselves.

Listening

Listening is one of the most important ways we reduce uncertainty because the law of uncertainty motivates us to listen so we know what is happening around us. Listening provides us with the information we need to make decisions in order to function on a daily basis. It is necessary not only for survival, but also for enjoyment, gaining information, and understanding others.

When we share meaning we not only communicate with one another, we need to listen to one another. Listening can communicate many things such as consideration, concern, empathy, friendship, and respect. We interpret not only what people say, but also the sounds we hear in the environment around us by investing them with meaning. We give meaning to words, the sounds around us, music, noises, and many other things we hear.

We are motivated by the law of investing to listen to others so that we can invest our time and resources in relationships with them. We place a value on listening and when we listen to others we show that we value them and what they have to say. When others listen to us we feel closer and more connected to them. Because listening takes time and energy, when we listen to others we may expect to receive something in return. We might expect that they will reciprocate and listen to what we have to say.

Listening is what makes the process of communicating work because it is an important connection by which we share our Great Idea with others and they provide us with feedback. When we communicate our Great Idea with others, we expect them to listen to us. Conversely, when they communicate with us to provide feedback, they expect that we will listen to them.

Listening is an important part of getting feedback from others because it is how we know if our message has been received and understood. By listening, we adjust our frame of reference to focus on what others have to say. We avoid filtering out information by paying attention to them. It is the means by which we understand and comprehend the feedback they provide.

Just as everyone communicates for reason, everyone listens for a reason. So, when you communicate with others, give them a reason to listen to you. When you listen let people know that they are important to you, that you respect their ideas, and that you are willing to consider what they have to say.

Language

Language is the system of spoken and written words we use to communicate with one another. It is a specific means of communicating where symbols, that are invested with meaning and shared by a people. In order for language to work, everyone has to agree on what the symbols mean and how to use them. Language is one of the single most important human creations. While language is something all people have in common, all people do not share a common language. Different groups of people have developed their own specialized ways of communicating based upon their ethnicity, culture, profession, or geographic affiliation.

The advantage of language is in its ability to convert everything we know and experience into symbols that can be easily shared by large numbers of people over vast distances. It gives us the ability to share, store, and transmit large quantities of information relatively easily. The power of language is in its ability to affect how we think and how it motivates our behavior. It enables us to work with one another to accomplish things and achieve our desired outcomes. It is the means by which we define ourselves, others, and everything around us. It is how we learn about and make sense of ourselves and the world around us. Without language, life as we know it would not be possible.

The law of uncertainty motivated people to develop language as an effective way to communicate with one another to reduce uncertainty about themselves, others, and the world around them. We use language to share information about ourselves in order to reduce uncertainty, to get to know other people, to create relationships, and to work together to get things done. It is how we share information and knowledge enabling us to learn from one another as well as about one another. Without language, life would have more uncertainty making society as we know it virtually impossible.

Language is the practical application of the law of shared meaning because it provides people a means to share their ideas with others. It allows people to share information and ideas that cannot be done in any other way. While pictures or drawings allow us to share some meaning, it's difficult or impossible to effectively communicate abstract and complex ideas using anything other than language. Language allows us to share meaning one on one or with large audiences. It allows us to transcend boundaries by sharing meaning with people across great distances and over time.

Language enables the law of investing to work because it is the means by which we take symbols and invest them with meaning. This gives us the ability to communicate and to invest in relationships with one another. It provides a means to measure everything around us and communicate its value.

Language can create power because it enables us to exercise control over resources and people. We can take large complex ideas and condense them into relatively small amounts of space, creating virtually unlimited numbers of copies, and distribute them to as many people as we like in order to send and receive information effectively and economically.

How we use language tells us what is important and what is not, what we value and what we don't. How we label things influences our perceptions and expectations of their past, present, and future value. Language creates many kinds of value; historical value, social value, cultural value, and monetary value. We use language to make value judgments about things by describing them as good or bad, rare or common, and expensive or cheap. This means that how we use language can have tangible results.

Language is the means by which we create and share social reality. When we communicate with one another and share stories about our experiences, we create a common culture. We use language to communicate our self-concept including our nationality, ethnicity, culture, and geographic affiliation. It is how we take ideas and communicate them to others in order to make them a reality. It is how we create and enforce the rules of society. It provides a means by which we make sense of ourselves, others, and the world around us.

Language has the ability to create and change people's perceptions and expectations. We use language to label things in order to shape physical reality. Language is an important part of the perception process that helps to create our expectations. We use language to share information about ourselves in order to influence people's perception of us. What we tell people affects their expectations about us in the future. This helps us to create and maintain relationships with one another.

Language allows us to share meaning that makes traditions and rituals more meaningful. This can make us feel closer and more connected to others, even with people we do not know. When we practice them we often say the same words and phrases as people practiced them in the past. Doing this gives us a sense of purpose, togetherness, and connectedness with a larger community.

For instance, when we go to Christmas services, they may have the same program that has been performed for many years. When we hear the same language spoken during celebrations at important times of the year it can give us a feeling of comfort and support for one another. This can help us to have a sense of security and stability.

Language can shape our behavior. Think about the last time you heard a passionate speech, read an inspirational poem, watched an emotional movie, or heard the lyrics to a sad song. It probably created feelings that affected your emotions. Language can create emotions that move people to take action to do things.

Throughout history, language has been used for gaining political, economic, and social power. It is a means to persuade people to accept new ideas and to be motivated to take action. We use language to shape people's perceptions and expectations. It is used to influence, motivate, and persuade us to take action. It has the power to shape how we perceive ourselves, others, and the world around us.

Language can shape our thoughts. It is flexible enough to enable us to think abstractly about things we can't see or that don't exist in reality. However, language can limit our ideas to the words that are available for us to use.

For instance, do you think about things using words or pictures? If we think in words, they could constrain our thoughts and ideas because we have to use the words that are available to us. The words available to us may or may not accurately express our ideas.

If we think in pictures or concepts, it may be difficult to put those ideas into words to communicate them to others. This brings up the problem of limitations with language. How would you use language to communicate about something that does not exist when there may be no words to describe it?

Language is a means of creative expression. It is not just a means to communicate ideas, it is also used as a means of entertainment and artistic creative self expression. It fulfills our need to express ourselves artistically and creatively. Language is used as a means of entertainment through comedy, drama, mystery, and suspense. Language makes drama, film, television, theater, music, opera, poetry, literature, and many other types of creative artistic expression possible. Language has the power to make us feel a wide variety of emotions. It can influence and inspire us.

Language can affect our emotions. Since words have meaning and meanings create emotions, words create feelings within us. Language can have a cathartic affect because it allows us to talk about how we feel providing an emotional release to make us feel better. Conversely, we can also use language to hide how we really feel.

Language can communicate who we are. It can communicate information about who we are as an individual. It can be a source of confidence, competence, attitudes, and preferences that can help to develop our self-concept and sense of identity. We use it to create our identity and manage how others perceive us. It can communicate the groups that we belong to including our profession, ethnicity, education, and geographic affiliation.

We use language to share information about ourselves including our experiences, interests, thoughts, and emotions. It is the means by which we think thoughts in order to develop our ideas. It enables us to think abstractly outside the limitations of time and space. It has the power to influence and persuade others how to think about things and motivate them to take action.

Language is about making choices and the choices people make communicate who they are as a person and how they want to be perceived by others. Language has the power to engage our minds and touch our hearts.

Nonverbal Communicating

Verbal communicating consists of both spoken and written language. Nonverbal communicating consists of practically everything else. We use nonverbal information to help us reduce uncertainty. It helps us to understand other people, their motives, and actions to make them seem safe and predictable. We do this so that we can trust them to invest in relationships.

When we want to know more about others, we look for meaning in the nonverbal information they communicate. This includes their appearance, demeanor, gestures, actions, behavior, and facial expressions. We look at how they use their resources such as how they spend their time, how they utilize their space, and the personal choices they make. All of these have the potential to communicate information nonverbally.

How we utilize nonverbal behavior is a practical application of the law of shared meaning. Uncertainty motivates us to invest nonverbal behavior with meaning so that we can better understand it. We use nonverbal behavior to convey meanings that language cannot adequately communicate. We use it to add additional meaning to what we say.

For example, if someone says, "Love you," the nonverbal information that accompanies it tells us how to interpret it. A smile may indicate friendship, a hug may indicate a family relationship, and a kiss may indicate a more intimate relationship.

We invest nonverbal behavior with meaning because there are many aspects to a person that we cannot directly observe. We cannot see their attitudes, experiences, motivations, desired outcomes, needs and wants, or view of social reality. If we do not have a complete picture of them, we might add information to fill in what is missing, which may or may not be accurate. This is why people often make assumptions about others that they know little about, which may not be true.

In order to invest in relationships with others, we need to reduce uncertainty to create trust. To do this, we observe and interpret a person's nonverbal behavior to give us information about them. This includes not only what they say, but how they say it. We also look at other nonverbal characteristics like their behavior, appearance, clothing, possessions, and how they organize their space at home and at work. We invest meaning in the things created by people such as clothing, furniture, art, music, literature, and architecture as well as others.

The more we invest in a relationship, the more kinds of nonverbal behavior we use to communicate. We use nonverbal communicating to signify our investment in relationships such as the use of facial expressions to indicate friendship or touch to express affection. We can use spatial relationships to indicate the nature of our relationships. We use food to welcome friends and family. We surround ourselves with objects we enjoy looking at, to create a pleasant atmosphere.

In the process of communicating, we make a connection with others to share our Great Idea and they provide us with feedback. Some of the feedback is nonverbal information based upon the behavior of others when they communicate with us. We often look for nonverbal feedback while we are talking with others to know if they understand what we are saying.

We look for facial expressions such as smiling or behavior like head nodding that indicates their approval. If we see negative feedback such as avoiding eye contact or negative facial expressions, we may not feel good about what we are saying and may stop to ask them what's the problem.

The nonverbal feedback we receive from others can have an impact on our self-concept because we view it as more instantaneous and honest. People have time to think about what they're going to say and so they may not be as forthright. They usually don't have time to think about how to act. People may say that they agree with us, but their nonverbal body language may say otherwise, so we are more likely to believe that. People may hold back and not say anything in response to us. However, they cannot hold back communicating nonverbally.

This is why we often look for nonverbal feedback as an indicator of how we are being perceived by others. Through the process of communicating, reflected feedback has the potential to have an effect on our self-concept.

Health and Uncertainty

Communicating effectively with others can help to create and maintain positive relationships to improve the quality of our health. This helps reduce uncertainty, which can improve blood pressure, reduce hypertension, and lower the risk of heart disease.

When we share meaning with others it can make us feel needed and appreciated. This helps to create and maintain relationships that provide us with support and nurturing. By developing communicating skills, we can gain many health benefits from uncertainty reduction.

The laws of uncertainty, shared meaning, and investing can help to diagnose and treat physical and mental health issues. For instance, in diagnosing illness we look for the cause or symptoms in order to find a treatment. However, there could be a deeper, underlying cause.

Increased uncertainty has the potential to be an underlying cause of health problems. So, when we treat the symptoms, it may help to look for ways to reduce uncertainty, share meaning, and encourage investing. Increased uncertainty can lead to stress, anxiety, and depression that can in turn affect our health and well being in many ways. Our mental state can affect our physical state. Many of the emotions we feel like anxiety, fear, and anger can have health consequences.

So, uncertainty has the potential to be an underlying source of medical and psychological conditions because social reality can create physical reality. For instance, someone may have a sleep or digestive disorder that is caused by stress or anxiety.

Their mental state may be manifesting itself in a physical malady caused by uncertainty at home or work. So, in diagnosing medical problems, it can be helpful to look at how the law of uncertainty may be affecting them.

The law of shared meaning can affect our relationships with others, which can affect how we see ourselves, our self-concept, and how we relate to others. So, the nature of our relationships can affect our health. For instance, if we have a good communicating network and support system, it can improve our confidence and self-concept, which can help us feel better.

If we share little meaning with others, we might feel alone, withdrawn, or depressed. If we are having difficulties in our relationships, it could diminish our confidence and self-concept. These can affect our health because psychological perceptions can have physical consequences.

The law of investing motivates us to invest in relationships with others to fulfill needs and wants we cannot fulfill ourselves. We invest in relationships because they can make us feel good about ourselves bolstering our self-concept, which can improve our health.

We also need to invest in ourselves, which includes both our physical and mental well being. While we maintain our possessions like a car or house, it is all too easy to neglect taking care of our most important asset, ourselves.

Good health is one of our most important needs and we want to feel good. Health and well being needs and wants can motivate behavior, however, the need to be healthy and wanting to feel good can be one of the most challenging set of conflicting needs and wants we have, making it difficult to find a balance.

For instance, we enjoy eating food that tastes good, but we also need to eat healthy, which may not be as satisfying. A person may feel depressed or stressed due to increased uncertainty or if their perceptions do not meet their expectations. This can motivate them to eat, drink, or smoke to feel better even though it is harmful to their health.

Our perceptions and expectations can also have an effect on our health. When our perceptions are accurate and our expectations are reasonable, we can feel good. When there is an uncomfortable level of uncertainty, we can be more prone to alcohol or drug abuse, fatigue, overeating, or other unhealthy behaviors.

However, if our perceptions are not meeting our expectations it can make us feel sad, depressed, or even angry, which can affect our mental as well as physical health. Treating health issues can include addressing psychological issues that can originate in uncertainty, perceptions and expectations, and needs and wants fulfillment.

Improving our awareness can help us to know more about our current state of health and what might happen in the future. Health care is one source of uncertainty because everyone will likely face health issues at sometime in their life. Increased awareness can help give us more options to prepare for and deal with them.

Improved awareness can help reduce the likelihood of having a health crisis because we can be better prepared for what might happen. Having options can help us to find the best possible solutions to potential health problems in order to improve our quality of life.

Uncertainty and Individual Communicating

There are times when we say something that makes us wonder why we said it. There are times we behave in ways that make us wonder if we really know who we are. We may feel tension or frustration and not really understand why.

By understanding how communicating works, we can more fully understand the forces that affect what we say and do. By understanding how we communicate with ourselves, we can make informed choices rather than letting uncertainty control us.

By understanding our needs and wants, we can know what motivates us. This can help us to simplify our life by focusing on the things that are important while discarding those that are not.

By increasing our knowledge of how the perception process, expectations, and desired outcomes work, we can better understand why we feel the way we do.

By understanding how the process of communicating works, we can develop skills to communicate more effectively with others improving how we see ourselves and our self-concept.

We can utilize the laws of uncertainty, shared meaning, and investing to better understand the forces that motivate us. These elements can be utilized as a diagnostic methodology to provide insights into ourselves.

We can identify sources of uncertainty in our lives to determine which ones we can do something about and what to do about them, as well as those that we can do little about in order to mitigate their effect on us.

We can increase our awareness of the meanings that we share with others and how they develop our social reality, as well as how they create our perception of ourselves, others, and the world around us.

Chapter 4
Relational Communicating

Throughout our life we are constantly meeting new people and developing new relationships while others fade away. This process is such a natural part of life we usually don't pay much attention to it because we are constantly going through the process of forming, maintaining, and ending relationships. So, what would you do if you had to form all new relationships?

Relational communicating is the second level of interaction because it is about how you communicate with others to create and maintain relationships. We use the word relationship to characterize the connections we make with others like our friends, family, spouses, coworkers, and business associates.

We might refer to a passing acquaintance as a relationship. We may talk about having a good relationship with a neighbor, coworker, or store clerk. However, when we do this we are referring to the positive climate of the interaction rather than making an ongoing reciprocated connection. We make connections and communicate with others all the time without forming an actual relationship.

We are motivated to form relationships by the law of uncertainty. When we don't know someone there is a high degree of uncertainty because we don't know what to expect from them. They probably feel the same because they do not know what to expect from us. We may perceive them as uncertain because we do not know if they will help or harm us.

When we reduce uncertainty we create security and stability making it easier for us to communicate with them. This builds trust making it easier for us to develop relationships with them. This process is necessary in order for society to function because if we didn't get to know people and develop trusting relationships with them, it would be nearly impossible to work together to get things done.

Relationships can create their own specialized social reality facilitated by the law of shared meaning. When two people make a connection to communicate with one another they often tell stories about themselves, talk about their experiences, and share their perceptions and expectations of themselves, others, and the things around them.

Sharing these things helps to promote increased understanding between them. Relationships do not exist in isolation. We have relationships with other people who in turn have relationships with others. This creates multiple connections that comprise networks of information that are communicated by people throughout society.

We are motivated by the law of investing to invest our time and other resources in others in order to gain rewards such as fulfilling our needs and wants. By getting to know others we can reduce uncertainty to help us trust them. The more we get to know someone, and the more they get to know us, the more likely we are to be comfortable investing in relationships with them. This is because when we get to know them we have reasonable expectations of their future behavior creating stability and predictability.

In relationships, we get to know what to reasonably expect from others and they get to know what they can reasonably expect of us. We are willing to make fair investments with the expectation of receiving fair rewards. We invest in relationships based upon our future expectations. If we have reasonable expectations of fair rewards that will fulfill our needs and wants, we can be willing to invest in a relationship even if it means putting off receiving benefits until sometime in the future. However, if our perception of what we are receiving does not meet our expectations it could undermine the relationship.

In the process of communicating, you create your Great Idea and communicate it to others across The Great Abyss. You do this by making connections with them. When you make a connection with another person, it can be the beginning of a relationship. This is because you have established your place in relation to the other person.

If the connection is reciprocated, a relationship can be created. However, not all communicating through connections will result in creating a relationship. If we do not make an ongoing connection with another person, then no relationship is created. Relationships are about the connections we make with others and the type of relationship is based upon the type of connection.

Relationships and the process of communicating can affect our self-concept because when we share meaning with others about our experiences, we also share meaning about ourselves. Our self-concept is created in part through reflective communicating. When we communicate our Great Idea to others they respond through feedback. The nature of their response can work like a mirror to communicate how they perceive us.

Since we cannot see ourselves as others see us, we utilize their feedback like a mirror to see ourselves. The information we receive can affect our self-concept. The closer the relationship and the better we know someone, the more likely we are to be aware of their feedback and utilize it. If we don't know someone very well, or the information we receive is too different from our own perception, we are more likely to brush it off or reject it.

Relationships are a natural and unavoidable part of life. We were created by nature with needs and wants, many of which we cannot fulfill ourselves. Without relationships, every time we had a need or want to fulfill, we would have to start over from the beginning. We would have to look for a way to fulfill it and find someone to help us do it. This motivates us to communicate with others in order to create and maintain relationships.

We create relationships with others based upon our perceptions of them and expectations of their future behavior. In relationships we have a perception of our own behavior including what we want to contribute as well as receive from the relationship. We have a perception of the other person's behavior and expectations, of what they contribute as well as what they receive from the relationship.

These perceptions and expectations may or may not accurately reflect reality. These perceptions are important because they can create satisfaction or dissatisfaction with the relationship. If we perceive that we are contributing more than the other person and they are receiving more benefits, we may feel we are being treated unfairly and become dissatisfied. Conversely, if we perceive that we are fairly contributing and receiving in a relationship, it can increase our relational satisfaction.

We have perceptions and expectations about all of our relationships whether we are aware of them or not. We may have realistic or unrealistic perceptions and expectations that can affect how we feel about our relationships and motivate our behavior. It can be helpful to be aware of our expectations and how they may be creating feelings of satisfaction or dissatisfaction.

This is because how we feel about our relationships can determine the commitment that we have to the other person and the relationship. This can happen whether we are aware of it or not, but by understanding how this process works, we can control it rather than let it control us, so we can have more satisfying relationships.

Having expectations helps us to invest in relationships because if we did not have any expectations we might be reluctant to invest because we would perceive them as too uncertain. We often take our perceptions and expectations for granted and do not communicate them clearly to others. In a relationship, it is easy to assume that the other person would just know what we want.

For example, in a romantic relationship one person might think that if the other person really loves them, they would know what they want. Since no two people have precisely the same perceptions and expectations, there is a good chance they don't know what you want. This can set up inaccurate expectations creating unnecessary unhappiness that can be resolved by clearly communicating your perceptions and expectations.

In order for relationships to function they need to be governed by a set of rules. If relationships did not have rules people would do whatever they felt like and things would become chaotic increasing uncertainty. These rules are often based upon a combination of the rules we get from our family, culture, ethnicity, religion, and geographic affiliation. These rules are important because they help people to know what is expected of them and what they can expect of others.

Rules can do this because they govern how people in a relationship communicate with one another as well as regulating their behavior. When others fulfill our expectations, we are more likely to reciprocate and follow the rules because they enable us to fulfill our needs and wants. When our perceptions of others do not meet our expectations, we are more likely to challenge or reject the rules because we may feel that they inhibit us from achieving our desired outcome.

When we first meet someone a relationship is governed by the rules of social reality. As we get to know them, a relationship begins to develop its own rules. Our behavior and how we communicate is determined by the nature of the relationship. As our relationship progresses we develop specialized rules that are more applicable to the nature of the relationship.

Conversely, the more impersonal the relationship, the more likely we are to continue to follow set patterns of communicating determined by social reality. For example, we often greet people by asking, "How are you?" The standard reply is to say that we are fine. When we get to know someone better, we might tell them how we really feel.

We develop rules in relationships based upon our past experiences. It is not uncommon for us to try to replicate what we perceive as a past success while avoiding past mistakes or repeating a bad experience. However, instead of helping a relationship, this could hinder or even undermine its success.

We are attracted to relationships when we know the rules. We are likely to be more attracted to relationships with others who we perceive as being similar to us because they share a similar set of rules, perceptions, expectations, and social reality. While this may be interpreted as being aloof or prejudicial, it is a natural response to uncertainty.

This is because sharing a similar social reality or set of rules helps to reduce uncertainty about others. Since a relationship is something that people create together, we are more likely to create relationships with others who share a similar social reality because it reduces uncertainty. If two people have conflicting social realities it can create obstacles that may be difficult to overcome impeding the establishment of a stable relationship.

Society places value on conformity because it creates stability, predictability, and reduces uncertainty, which is necessary for people to form relationships. Each person is expected to communicate and behave in certain ways, complete specific tasks, and follow the rules of the relationship if they want to receive its benefits. While this may seem restrictive, without rules uncertainty would be increased making it more difficult to maintain a relationship.

When we first meet someone and begin to develop a relationship the rules have not yet been fully established. This creates a sense of uneasiness or awkwardness we often experience when we first meet someone. In order to get things started, we rely on familiar patterns of communicating determined by the rules of social reality.

If we did not do this a high level of uncertainty would maintain feelings of uneasiness and awkwardness. This could prevent the relationship from functioning properly because no one would know what was expected of them or what to expect from others. While a high degree of uncertainty can create excitement in a new relationship, it can also become tiresome over time.

As we get to know others, we negotiate our own rules to govern the relationship. Most of the time these rules are communicated indirectly. We may only become aware of them after we have violated a rule and the other person gets upset with us. In order to avoid this, it is helpful to communicate perceptions and expectations about the relationship and its rules.

We form relationships because they can be fun and enjoyable. They can fulfill our need for affiliation and companionship because we like being around others. People can be interesting and entertaining fulfilling our need for excitement and variety. However, after a while a relationship may become more routine so it feels like hard work leaving us wondering what happened. This is because relationships are not just fun and enjoyable, they have tasks that must be accomplished and needs that must be fulfilled to function properly.

The social aspects of a relationship are important because nobody wants to work all the time, we want to enjoy things as well. Relationships help us to fulfill important social needs such as relaxation, escape, and pleasure. They help us to reduce tension and to share interests with others. Even in work situations where the focus is on getting tasks done, having social time is essential to healthy working relationships.

People need to take time off to get to know one another, to relieve stress, or just have fun. This is one reason why coworkers will socialize by going to lunch or out together after work. Regardless of the type of relationship, the functional aspect of getting things done and the social needs of the individuals should be addressed for the health of the relationship.

Variant Behavior

Have you ever felt like you acted in one way when you were with one person and in a distinctly different way when you were with someone else? We might change our behavior depending upon who we are with because of the effect that they have on us. This happens because we all have variable and nonvariable characteristics. Nonvariable characteristics include the things we cannot change about ourselves such as our gender, ethnicity, or age. These are the things about us that do not change when our circumstances change and they are the things that people are most likely to notice about us.

Variable characteristics include those things about us that we can change depending upon our circumstances. They can include things such as how outgoing we are, our sense of humor, or what we like to talk about. Variable behavior determines how we act differently when we are out with friends, at work, or in church.

Our behavior with others changes depending upon the nature of our relationship with them. There are characteristics of our personality that become dominant or regressive depending upon who we are with, the nature of the relationship, and the particular situation. We can do this in ways that we may not even notice. We may be outgoing and have a sense of humor when we are with our friends and act more subdued or serious with our coworkers at work.

How we communicate depends upon the nature of the relationship. What is acceptable in one relationship may be considered inappropriate in another. We may feel comfortable telling jokes or colorful stories with our friends, but not with our coworkers. This negotiated collective shared meaning that we develop with others can influence and motivate our behavior.

How we accomplish this depends on our past experiences, the nature of the relationship, and our desired outcome for forming the relationship. It is likely influenced by the perceptions and expectations that we have of ourselves and that others have of us. We do this to manage our identity and present ourselves in a manner that encourages development of the relationship.

We often behave differently in different relationships because they are created by the people involved in them. Every relationship has its own unique qualities that give it a distinctive character or personality. This means that it is possible for a relationship to become something that we do not want or do not intend it to be. This is why we may feel that a relationship is not going the way we want or that we don't have any control over it, because to some extent we don't.

How this works can be illustrated by imagining two musicians playing on the same street corner. If each of them are playing their own song it would be difficult to hear either one of them and it would probably sound awful. If they play the same song together it would sound much better.

However, neither one has complete control over what the people passing by hear. They hear a combination of the two that neither can create by themselves. When people in relationships behave as individuals, like the musicians, it can become hard work that can increase uncertainty. When people are aware of how relationships work they can work together to make the relationship less stressful, less work, and more beneficial to both.

Since every relationship is a separate entity created by the people involved, it can develop its own unique personality. This is because we manage our identity based upon our perceptions of how others perceive us and our expectations in the relationship.

Through the process of reflective feedback, other people can have an affect on our variable characteristics, which can change our behavior. Different people have the potential to bring out different parts of our personality. This is why we may act one way in one relationship and in an entirely different way in another. We may even act in ways we do not expect.

Since a relationship is a separate entity with its own unique characteristics it can develop its own rules, structure, and norms of behavior which may be the same or different than we have in our other relationships. We may find ourselves with one set of behavioral norms in one relationship and a different set in another, motivating us to exhibit different behaviors and communicate in different ways.

We manage our identity in our relationships, and in each relationship we make different choices how to do that. Since a relationship is a combination of the people who created it, even though it involves us, we might feel like we have little control over it and may be surprised by the direction it is going.

Gender

For many of our relationships gender is not a particularly significant factor because they are based upon what a person does or who they are. We may prefer to develop close personal relationships like friends of one gender over another. We choose partners or spouses based on gender.

Gender can be a source of uncertainty because when we perceive something as different it can create uncertainty. This can motivate us to want to know more, so we may spend time and effort trying to understand people based on their gender. We look for ways to understand others by looking at how they are different. We may assume that since there are physical differences, there must be other kinds of differences as well.

Since we are motivated to understand others better, we might concentrate more on differences rather than similarities. However, when it comes to communicating and behavior, we may actually be more similar than we are different. We may be finding differences simply because we expect them.

Much of what is considered to be masculine and feminine in behavioral communicating is determined by how people construct social reality. Our perceptions and expectations about gender have been developed over long periods of time. People follow familiar patterns of communicating based upon gender in order to fulfill these expectations. Relationships involve specialization of labor which determines who does what tasks. This specialization creates expectations contained in the rules of social reality that influence tasks in a relationship.

Relationships are formed to help fulfill our needs and wants. We often form gender based relationships to fulfill some of our most important needs and wants, giving us higher expectations about what we contribute and receive. These relationships often involve needs of closeness, affection, and intimacy.

This means that men and women can be motivated to communicate differently based on their needs and wants. They may have the perception that if they communicate based upon the expectations of others, they are more likely to achieve their desired outcomes. So, we have developed different styles of communicating and behavior based on gender in order to fulfill the expectations of others to fit in their social reality.

When we perceive the behavior of others, we can have a natural tendency to make generalizations in order to reduce uncertainty to make people more familiar. We do this on the basis of many characteristics such as a person's age, education, ethnicity, and gender. Social reality creates societal generalizations about different gender behaviors. A common generalization characterizes men as being aggressive or competitive and women as nurturing or domestic, even though they do not necessarily hold true.

We have expectations about how each gender communicates based upon the rules of social reality and what we consider to be masculine or feminine. These have become familiar, so we don't think much about them. Expectations influence our behavior and how we communicate with others. In order to form relationships and function in everyday activities, we are motivated to meet the expectations of others, so we often communicate with others based upon how we think we should communicate.

Communicative behavior is influenced by the rules of social reality, which exerts pressure on us to follow established patterns of communicating. These influence our perceptions and expectations about how each gender communicates. We communicate based upon those perceptions to fulfill the expectations of others. We are motivated to do this to manage our identity so that we will be accepted and fit in.

Much of how we perceive the differences in how gender is communicated comes from others around us and through the media. Social reality provides information that can form the basis of our expectations motivating people's behavior. So, do you communicate differently with people based on gender?

The law of shared meaning motivates us to find meaning in many things. We invest gender with meaning including what it means to be a man and what it means to be a woman. We interpret certain behaviors like body language and styles of communicating as masculine or feminine. We have expectations about what is appropriate clothing for each gender. Because our perception of gender is constructed by social reality it can transfer gender characteristics to inanimate objects.

From the time we are born we learn gender expectations from our parents and family based upon our culture, traditions, ethnicity, religion, and geographic affiliation. Different cultures, religions, and geographic areas have differing rules that define the roles of men and women. We learn this behavior by observing and imitating others we see around us.

From an early age people communicate with us differently based upon our gender because they are motivated to follow the rules, not only of social reality, but also their culture, ethnicity, religion, and family traditions. Since self-concept is partly developed through reflected communicating, these differences can become part of our self-concept affecting our behavior. These gender differences are often communicated from generation to generation so they can be slow to change.

We are motivated by the law of uncertainty to not deviate too much in our behavior from the expectations of others for fear that they will be less likely to form relationships with us. This is because when we communicate and behave in ways others expect, it reduces uncertainty, so they are more likely to form relationships that help us to fulfill our needs and wants. The perceptions of others have an impact on how we communicate and behave including how we are expected to behave based upon our gender. This can make gender communicating and behavior self replicating.

People who fit these expectations tend to be perceived with less uncertainty making it more likely for them to form relationships. So, we tend to modify our behavior to meet the expectations of others. Awareness helps us look at what we know in a new way to break typical patterns in how we communicate based on gender to develop ones based upon individual characteristics. Having options gives us different ways to communicate in order to determine the best one that works for each relationship.

Why we form relationships.

By forming relationships, we are able to communicate less superficially with others and interact with them on a deeper, more meaningful level. We can communicate with them in a way that would be considered uncomfortable and inappropriate if we did not have a relationship with them. This is necessary in order to more fully understand ourselves, others, and our experiences. It helps us to know more about ourselves and others to reduce uncertainty. It provides useful information in order to enable self-improvement and personal growth.

We are motivated to form relationships in order to achieve desired outcomes we cannot achieve on our own. These can include things like being on a sports team, finding a job, or getting married. We develop professional relationships to earn income necessary to help us fulfill our monetary needs. We develop personal relationships to help fulfill our social needs such as being part of a group. We develop intimate relationships to help fulfill our needs for closeness and intimacy. When we form relationships it provides benefits for others as well as ourselves.

Relationships help us to fulfill our needs and wants. When we are born, our family provides for all our needs. As we get older, we develop our own relationships to help us to obtain the things we need like a job, family, home, and even a positive self-concept. Without relationships, achieving these outcomes would be more difficult, if not impossible.

Relationships can be used to gain power, status, and respect. Developing relationships can be used to elevate a person's status so they are perceived as being important to others. This can help to provide them with resources to achieve their desired outcomes. Relationships can help us to exercise control not only over our lives, but also over resources and the actions of others.

We are motivated to form relationships in order to fulfill needs and wants we cannot fulfill ourselves. Relationships provide a consistent means of needs and wants fulfillment. They motivate us to take action and get to know others rather than living by ourselves in a cabin in the woods. We do this because if we had to negotiate with someone every time we needed something it would take too much time and energy. Relationships provide us with connections on an ongoing basis making a more efficient use of our time and resources.

Relationships help provide us with feedback. When we develop a relationship with others, we may feel comfortable sharing our thoughts and feelings with them. This is because we feel comfortable being ourselves so we can more easily talk about things without having to worry about what we say or how they will react.

We communicate our thoughts and feelings in order to gain new insights into ourselves from others we cannot gain by ourselves. This is because when we share ideas with others they add their perceptions and experiences that give our ideas additional meaning. They can also give us advice on how we can improve because they see us from a different perspective that we cannot see ourselves.

Relationships contribute to the development of our self-concept. Our self-concept is partially constructed through reflective communicating with others. We utilize feedback from others to create a picture of how they perceive us. This can be helpful in managing our identity and communicating more effectively with others.

This is why it is important to create relationships with others who will be honest with us, so that we can trust their feedback. This information can help us to improve ourselves and our communicating skills. However, we can be motivated to seek relationships with others who will simply confirm our own perception of ourselves, which may or may not be accurate.

We form relationships to provide support because life can be challenging, discouraging, and difficult. We form relationships to help make life easier and the workload lighter. Relationships make us feel that the problems of life are not so difficult because they provide us with both tangible and emotional support.

Relationships make us feel valued because others invest in us by contributing their time and other resources. We feel valued because we are part of someone else's life. This is because they take an interest in what we do, what we think, and how we feel. We feel a sense of attachment because having connections with others validates our own existence. Relationships can bolster our self-concept because we feel better about ourselves when we are appreciated by others.

Relationships make life more meaningful because we share thoughts, ideas, feelings, and emotions to gain a different perspective giving them a deeper meaning. Our experiences can be more fun when we share them with others. Our ideas are more interesting when others appreciate them. Perhaps these are some of the reasons why nature created us with needs and wants we cannot fulfill ourselves, so that we are motivated to form relationships with others.

How we form relationships.

While we could potentially meet anyone to develop a relationship, we only make connections with a limited number of people and most of them never develop into relationships because we have a limited amount of time and energy to invest in them. We cannot form a relationship with someone without first making a connection. The most common ways we meet people are those who we see on a regular basis through everyday activities such as work, school, church, in our community, or doing errands. The closer their proximity, the greater the frequency, and the more intense the connection, the greater the likelihood of developing a relationship.

Family is the most common form of group. These are the people we are related or close to and the first people with whom we develop relationships. Because of the close ties, these relationships are often the strongest and last the longest. Family relationships are generally structured and have specific labels such as parent, child, or sibling. These relationships have a formal aspect that carries societal and legal expectations such as a parent, child, or spouse. However, each family can develop their own ways of expressing these relationships.

Professional relationships are the next most common. Some of our closest relationships are often developed through our work because we spend the most time there away from home. We are motivated to create relationships at work to get along with our coworkers and help us do our job better. It is easy to create relationships with people from work because we are in close proximity, we spent a lot of time together, and we often have much in common with them such as similar knowledge and experiences. We develop professional relationships to make work easier or to help our career. However, just like relationships created by short periods of intensity, if we leave our job, our work relationships are likely to fade away unless there is another connection to sustain them.

Proximity is probably the single most important factor in developing relationships. Proximity involves people who are close to us, who share the same geographic or professional space like our family, friends, neighbors, or coworkers. In order to have a relationship with someone, we first have to meet them. We cannot have relationships with people we've never met because we need to make a connection with them. Typically, we meet someone face to face, but we can also develop relationships in other ways such as by mail, telephone, or over the internet.

We not only have to make a connection with someone, we have to keep in contact with them. Frequency is how often we see someone or communicate with them over a period of time. We can develop relationships with people who are not in close proximity, but with whom we have frequent contact. The more we communicate with someone, the higher the likelihood we self-disclose information about ourselves increasing the potential of creating a relationship.

Intensity is the degree of contact we have with someone over a period of time. If we see someone frequently or spend a large amount of time with them, the intensity of the contact can help to create a relationship. Our most intense relationships are often with the people we see where we live and work. We can also meet someone and spent a lot of time with them, however, a short intense relationship tends to not last very long because when the intensity subsides, the relationship is not as sustainable.

Similarity and the law of uncertainty motivate people to create and maintain relationships with people who they perceive as similar because uncertainty is reduced. Similarity can include many qualities such as similar likes, dislikes, interests, education, or work. It can be with people who share similar values, attitudes, or beliefs. We are more likely to create relationships with people who have similar backgrounds like culture, education, ethnicity, or geographic affiliations. They may have similar tastes in food, clothing, or music. They may have similar experiences, occupation, or participate in the same activities that we do. The more we find someone is similar to ourselves, the more we have to talk about so we can utilize the law of shared meaning to create interest in a relationship.

Some relationships form when we meet new people through someone we already know. The people we know also have friends, family, coworkers, and acquaintances. They may introduce us to someone with whom we develop our own relationship. These relationships reduce uncertainty because we both know the same person so we already have something in common. The rationale is that relationships should have a degree of transitivity. For instance, if we are friends with person A, and they are friends with person B, then we should be able to be friends with person B.

Since relationships are created between the people involved, this does not necessarily hold true. Just because one person we like is friends with someone, it does not necessarily mean we will like them or they will like us. This is why some people may be reluctant to introduce us to people they know because if it doesn't turn out well, they may be afraid that we will blame them or it could hurt their other relationships. Alternately, their friend may end up liking us better changing or ending our friend's relationship with their friend. It might also change or end our relationship with our friend as well.

Common ground is formed when we meet someone we look for things we have in common to feel comfortable with them. Finding common ground gives us familiar topics of conversation to make connections with others to share meaning, which reduces uncertainty. This increases the likelihood of developing a relationship because it bolsters our self-concept making us feel more comfortable around others. We are more likely to develop relationships with people we find interesting and can engage in conversation. Conversely, we are less likely to develop relationships with people that are difficult to talk to or we perceive as not interesting.

Attraction helps to form relationships with others because we like to be around people we find attractive and those who find us attractive. We find others attractive for many reasons other than just physical appearance. Attraction can be intellectual, emotional, professional, or psychological depending upon our needs and wants.

We are attracted to others because we find them exciting, interesting, considerate, supportive, or stable. We are attracted to people who like us, who make us feel important, who bolster our self-concept, and make us feel attractive. Attraction is a powerful motivating force because it represents our expectations of fulfilling future needs and wants. The perception of attractiveness can determine whether or not we pursue a relationship.

We like people who like us and likeability is about how others perceive us. We like people who like us because they have good taste. They make us feel good about ourselves and bolster our self-concept. Since our self-concept is enhanced through reflective feedback, when we are liked by others we feel accepted and valued as a person.

Being liked is a powerful social reward. When someone likes us it helps to reduce uncertainty and makes us feel more at ease. Conversely, the lack of approval can be used as a punishment. If someone doesn't like us it can increase tension because no one likes to be around someone who doesn't like them.

Every once in awhile we meet someone by random chance and hit it off, becoming friends or perhaps more. When we meet them we may feel a connection, a gut feeling, or intuition that peaks our interest motivating us to pursue a relationship. These types of relationships can surprise us because they tend to go against typical methods of forming relationships due to their high degree of uncertainty.

Identity Management

Identity management comprises the choices we make about what we say and how we behave when we communicate with others. It would be extremely difficult as well as rather unwise to try to communicate everything about ourselves because it would be overwhelming and inappropriate. Therefore, we need to make choices about what information we communicate about ourselves, to whom, and under what circumstances. Identity management works like public relations, we make choices about what information we communicate to others that can shape their impression of us and to help us achieve our desired outcomes.

When we meet other people, we communicate information about ourselves whether we choose to or not. We may choose what to say, but we cannot choose to stop communicating nonverbally. How others perceive us, as well is how we perceive ourselves, is partially based upon our individual characteristics.

Others use these characteristics to gather information about us in order to reduce uncertainty to determine how to behave. This is due to our natural tendency to want to understand others and their motivations based upon observable characteristics. We make inferences about others based upon many characteristics such as their age, gender, ethnicity, height, weight, clothing, possessions, and appearance.

We make perceptual inferences based upon these characteristics motivated by the law of shared meaning. People look for meaning in what they perceive about others. They do this by comparison, they take what they observe and compare it to their past experiences. People do this because it is an easy way to gain information about others rather than doing the more difficult task of finding things out for themselves.

Identity management is to some extent based upon the perceptions and expectations of others. Motivated by the law of uncertainty, we may choose to communicate only certain information and alter our behavior in order to be perceived as being like others so we will be accepted by them. If we act too differently from our true selves, identity management might be perceived as manipulation or phony.

Conversely, low degrees of identity management could communicate the impression that we don't care about ourselves or others. Identity management is a matter of balance. It can be helpful to use an appropriate level of identity management to maintain your individuality, while being considerate of the expectations of others.

Identity management is governed by the law of investing because we invest part of ourselves and our resources to get to know others. We are careful about how much information we share and our level of investment, so that we get what we expect in return. If we do achieve a portion of our desired outcome, we are more likely to share more later. If not, we may be less likely to put ourselves out again in the future.

We communicate for a reason so we create identities for a reason. We do this to fit in with the expectations of others to reduce uncertainty, so that they will be willing to invest in relationships with us. People do not want to be around or invest their time in others whose behavior they perceive as unpredictable because there is too much uncertainty.

People like to be around others who they perceive as being stable and predictable, so they can trust them because they know what they can reasonably expect in the future.

Relational Development

All relationships have one thing in common, at one time the people involved did not know each other. This means that relationships go through the process of relational development. This process can be characterized by four phases that are governed by the laws of uncertainty, shared meaning, and investing.

Since everyone is different there is no one right way to develop a relationship. A relationship can go through these phases rather quickly or it might take some time. How a relationship goes through these phases depends on the nature of the relationship, the individuals involved, and their desired outcomes.

1. Relational creation is how we form relationships. This is the law of uncertainty phase because we get to know others by reducing uncertainty.

2. Relational growth is how we develop relationships. This is the law of shared meaning phase because we share meaning through the process of self-disclosure to develop commitment to the relationship.

3. Relational maintenance is how we sustain relationships over time. This is the law of investing phase because it is when we invest our time, energy, and other resources in maintaining the relationship.

4. Relational dissolution is how relationships end. This is a return to the law of uncertainty phase because uncertainty in the relationship is increased to the point of breaking it apart.

I. Relational Creation, The Law Of Uncertainty Phase

When we first meet someone we may be unsure of how to communicate with them. So, we rely on familiar patterns of communicating governed by the rules of social reality to tell us how to behave. We use the perception process to obtain information about them in order to help us know how to proceed. Based on the information we have, we try different approaches looking for one that will work. This is why there is often an awkward tension or stiffness when we first meet someone, because we feel self conscious, perhaps even uncomfortable not knowing what to do or what to expect from them. So, before we can form a relationship uncertainty needs to be reduced.

The first phase of relational development is motivated by the law of uncertainty. The first time people get together is generally based upon the connections they have with one another. They may communicate with one another because they are in close proximity, have similarities, communicate frequently, or share common interests. They may seek to form relationships in order to fulfill needs and wants they cannot fulfill themselves.

Whenever we encounter a new situation that we are unfamiliar with, we look for ways to communicate with others. If we had to figure out how to communicate in each and every situation it would take too much time and energy. So, as part of the rules of social reality people have developed patterns of communicating that tell them how to act and behave in various situations. These are predetermined ways we communicate with others that work like a script in a play or movie. We use them because everyone knows the lines and what to expect, reducing uncertainty.

Behavioral reinforcement.

We use behavioral reinforcement to reduce uncertainty about others in order to invest in relationships with them. We communicate by utilizing the process of communicating to make a connection with them to share our Great Idea. Then we wait for feedback to know how well it was received. Their feedback can shape the nature of the relationship.

When we first communicate with someone we can potentially receive one of three responses. Our message is either accepted, rejected, or ignored. If we receive positive feedback then our message is accepted and we are on our way to developing a relationship. If we do something that is successful we are likely to repeat it. When something results in a successful outcome we are more comfortable with it because it reduces uncertainty.

This can make us more likely to take the same approach in other situations because we now have reasonable expectations that it will work again. However, over time things change, so past ways of communicating may become less effective and eventually no longer work. Rather than looking for a new approach, we might keep trying the old ones that could make things worse. Eventually past approaches may no longer work making us wonder what went wrong. What we need to do is examine our perceptions and expectations, gather fresh information, and create a new approach.

When we receive negative feedback, we might feel that not only is our message rejected, we may also feel personally rejected as well. We may try a different approach and if we receive negative feedback again, we may become frustrated or agitated reducing the likelihood of future contact. This can discourage us from communicating or behaving in this way again because it was unsuccessful. It may have a negative impact on our self-concept and we may even feel hurt or rejected. Since these feelings are uncomfortable, we are less likely to repeat them in the future. However, negative feedback can sometimes be perceived as a challenge encouraging some people to try it again, sometimes acting out more forcefully.

If feedback is ambiguous or unclear it can motivate us to repeat the original message until we get a clear reply. However, the other person may choose to ignore us by providing no feedback. This can be the most difficult response to deal with because there is no information to interpret. We cannot be sure if the other person was unable to respond or just didn't care. With no information we often provide our own interpretation perhaps deciding it is not worth the effort. If we feel there's something to be gained, we may continue to repeat the message until we get either positive or negative feedback.

II. Relational Growth, The Law Of Shared Meaning Phase

The second phase of relational development is motivated by the law of shared meaning because we need to share meaning in order to grow a relationship. In this phase, the uncertainty that creates the awkwardness and stiffness we feel when we first meet someone is reduced so that a relationship can be formed.

When individuals are comfortable being around each other, they begin to talk about themselves and share stories about their past experiences. The process of self-disclosure helps to develop trust so a relationship can share meaning.

Since a relationship is a separate entity created by the individuals involved, each person has only partial control over it. So, it can have characteristics similar to an individual, but function like a separate entity with a unique personality that may differ from the people involved. This is one reason why people often talk about a relationship as if it's another person.

A relationship is created utilizing the law of shared meaning based on the connections between people. This motivates them to self-disclose, so that they can better understand each other and communicate more effectively. This helps them to create a shared history, traditions, rituals, and behaviors. People create connections with others to communicate what the relationship means to them and what it means to be in the relationship.

When we first meet someone, we know little or nothing about them creating a high degree of uncertainty. In order to develop a relationship, we need to reduce uncertainty enough to feel comfortable communicating information about ourselves to the other person. This is done through self-disclosure, which is the process by which we share or disclose information about ourselves with others. It is how we share meaning to develop relationships because it is a more personal form of communicating than conversation.

It would be almost impossible to develop meaningful relationships without self-disclosure because it helps to develop trust. When we know more about others it increases our ability to trust them because it reduces uncertainty by sharing meaning. If this does not happen the relationship may not develop.

Self-disclosure is important to relational development because it helps to reduce uncertainty about others. We expect others to reciprocate by disclosing the same kinds of information that we disclose to them. If they do, we feel more comfortable with them because they are willing to contribute to the relationship.

Self-disclosure reduces tension because there is less uncertainty and we feel more safe and secure around them. The nature of the information they share can be a measure of the degree that they trust us and their expectations about the relationship.

Self-disclosure can be one way that we actualize the law of shared meaning. When we self-disclose we tell stories about ourselves, our experiences, things we have done, and people we have known. This helps others to relate their own experiences giving our stories additional meaning. When we share our experiences, we create common bonds that help to build relationships. Doing this gives our experiences deeper meaning when we add their perspective to ours.

Self-disclosure is governed by the rules of social reality. In order for this process to work, it's helpful to be aware of how it can help us create positive relationships. It is customary to share basic information about our self with others without going into great detail. As we get to know someone, we share more personal information about ourselves.

III. Relational Maintenance, The Law Of Investing Phase

We often hear that relationships like marriage can be hard work. Tasks need to be accomplished and things need to be done in order to maintain a relationship, but should it be hard work? Instead, it could be energizing and invigorating, because if the work is too hard we may decide it's not worth it and the relationship could deteriorate or come to an end.

Relational maintenance is the third phase of relational development. It is about making a commitment to keep a relationship together over time. It is motivated by the law of investing because we need to invest ourselves in our relationships in order to maintain them.

Our relational satisfaction is based upon our perceptions and expectations. People have a perception of their relationships that includes what they are willing to contribute based upon their expectations of future benefits. It can be helpful to talk about your perceptions and expectations and how the relationship is fulfilling your mutual needs, wants, and desired outcomes.

The power of the laws of uncertainty, shared meaning, and investing can be utilized for effective relational maintenance. Developing effective communicating skills can reduce uncertainty to help us feel more safe and secure increasing stability and commitment to the relationship.

However, some uncertainty can provide excitement to keep a relationship fun and interesting. Individuals use shared meaning to better understand one another by sharing their thoughts and feelings through appropriate ongoing self-disclosure.

They share their experiences to give them deeper meaning. The law of investing motivates people to maintain their relationships by investing in one another for their mutual benefit to achieve their desired outcomes. People form relationships to fulfill needs and wants, so how well they are fulfilled can determine their satisfaction and commitment to the relationship.

Relational commitment.

Relational commitment is the degree to which a person is willing to put the needs of the relationship ahead of their own. It's the degree to which people are willing to make sacrifices and do things for others and their relationship. It is the degree to which someone is willing to stay in a relationship regardless of how difficult things may get. Generally, the higher the level of the relationship, the higher the commitment.

However, there are times when this is not enough, even people in close, intimate relationships can breakup. If commitment is lacking in a relationship, it can be improved through the things that helped to form it in the first place like familiarity, intensity, frequency, and similarity. These help to bring people closer together. People in a relationship may slowly drift apart over time because they change, circumstances change, and their needs and wants change.

In the beginning, a relationship takes effort because it is new and exciting. When it has stabilized it feels secure, so we turn our attention to those things that are have a higher degree of uncertainty.

This is why over time relationships may have the feeling that one or both people are no longer as interested in the relationship or may take it for granted. However, this is probably not the case, it's more likely that other issues have not been resolved creating tension that takes more time and attention.

This situation can be improved by paying more attention to the needs and wants of the other person and the relationship. Instead of doing an occasional grand gesture, it's helpful to do little things more often that show your appreciation. Showing that you care does not have to be a lot of time consuming work, it can be expressed by doing little things every day.

IV. Relational Dissolution, Return To The Law Of Uncertainty Phase

The loss of a relationship is a consequence of the law of uncertainty. People may grow apart, their needs or wants may change, or they may have experienced something that is difficult to overcome. Relationships can end suddenly and unexpectedly or slowly drift away over time.

While we may have little or no control over some relationships, others may have warning signs that the relationship is in trouble giving us a chance to do something about it. If we are careful about maintaining a relationship, we can recognize problems and deal with them as they occur. If we avoid the warning signs, it can increase uncertainty creating unhappiness, misunderstandings, tension, and even conflict resulting in their deterioration or disillusion.

We form relationships in order to fulfill specific needs and wants. If those needs and wants are reasonably fulfilled, it provides an incentive to maintain the relationship. However, our needs and wants can change over time and so do our relationships. We may form a relationship based upon a specific need or want such as with our coworkers when we get a job.

These relationships fulfill our needs at the time, but if we leave our job the need no longer exists. If any of our work relationships have not made another connection or progressed to another level beyond the initial need or want, then there's no longer any need for these relationships to continue, so they may deteriorate or end.

Changes in relationships can make them more unstable leading to deterioration or dissolution. Things happen to us, people say and do things, and other people might get involved in a relationship that can increase uncertainty. The stronger the relationship, the more uncertainty it can withstand.

However, if the uncertainty becomes too great it can cause the relationship to deteriorate or dissolve. Relationships are based on creating common connections through shared meaning. If individuals in the relationship start sharing different meanings with others outside the relationship it could pull the relationship apart.

Uncertainty and Relational Communicating

Relationships can be difficult. People seem to do things for no apparent reason. We might feel that a relationship is not going right, or did not turn out like we had hoped. This can leave us feeling upset or frustrated and we may not know why.

By understanding how the laws of uncertainty, shared meaning, and investing affect us, we can better understand how relationships are created and maintained. We can develop skills to communicate effectively with others to improve our relationships.

We form relationships to fulfill needs and wants, and to achieve our desired outcomes. By having a clearer understanding of our own needs and wants, as well as those of others, we can better fulfill them and help others to fulfill theirs to have more satisfying relationships.

We can reduce uncertainty by utilizing the perception process to better understand ourselves, others, and our relationships. So, when they do not meet our expectations, instead of causing unnecessary tension and dissatisfaction, we have options to be more effective.

We can reduce uncertainty by understanding how we create relationships. We can grow our relationships through self-disclosure to share meaning with others to get to know them better.

We can invest in relationships to maintain them fostering a commitment to others. We can have options for handling difficult aspects of relationships, so when we have a conflict we can reach a more satisfying resolution.

This approach to uncertainty could be utilized as a diagnostic methodology to evaluate our relationships to improve them so they can be more satisfying. We can identify the relational skills that we have and those that could use improvement as a means to form better relationships. It can help us feel better about ourselves improving our self-concept and giving us more confidence in our relationships.

By understanding our desired outcomes in relationships, we can focus on what is really important to us and clarify our priorities in order to achieve them more effectively.

Chapter 5
Professional Communicating

Professional communicating is the third level of interaction. It is about how you communicate with others to create and maintain professional affiliations and other types of relationships in groups and organizations. It can characterize the connections we make with others including our friends, family, coworkers, colleagues, and business associates. Groups are important to us because they permeate practically all aspects of our lives.

We often define ourselves based upon the groups we belong to like our profession, religion, ethnicity, culture, and geographic affiliations such as where we live or were born. We identify with groups based on personal interests, hobbies, sports, work, and other activities. While many of these things are based on our individual interests, we do not do them by ourselves, but rather in groups with other people.

When you talk to other people, what do you tell them about yourself? You might say something like you play the guitar or are a football fan. You might say that you are a parent, a teacher, or play in a softball league. The first items are about you as an individual, but the second items are about your relationships with others in groups.

When we communicate with others, we manage our identity to shape their perception of us to achieve our desired outcomes. We use our group affiliations to define ourselves, to make connections, and to find common ground with others. We do this because groups are a part of our self-concept and how we define ourselves.

In order to increase your awareness of how groups affect you, it can be helpful to write down on a piece of paper all the groups that you have ever belonged to whether you are currently a member or not. Then write down why you joined each group and if that reason is still the same or has changed.

Groups and uncertainty.

We are motivated to form groups and organizations to reduce uncertainty about ourselves, others, and the world around us. Groups reduce uncertainty by fulfilling many of our needs and wants. They create stability, security, and predictability. They have longevity beyond their individual members.

Groups can acquire and allocate more resources than individuals. They can exert influence to regulate members' behavior. They let members know what is expected of them and what they can expect from others.

Groups share meaning about the group and what it means to be a member. They share meaning through traditions and rituals creating their own customs and culture. They may even have their own language, symbols, and terms. It is by being in groups that we get to know people through the process of self-disclosure. Sharing meaning helps people to reduce uncertainty, so they are better able to invest in the group and the other members. Groups help their members to invest in one another and provide a means to protect those investments.

Much of our life is organized based upon groups such as our family, work, school, church, and community. We invest our time, energy, and other resources in groups with the expectation that we will receive benefits for our contributions. Group members are more likely to share their resources with other group members including their time, energy, expertise, experience, and even material resources.

Groups allow for role specialization, so that each person can spend more time on specific parts of a task and learn specific skills they might not otherwise be able to do when working alone. Groups contribute to our self-concept and affect how others see us. They share meaning about the group and what it means to be a member.

Why we form groups.

Life can be chaotic and unpredictable. People behave in ways that seem unexpected, even threatening. We are motivated to form groups in order to reduce uncertainty about ourselves and others. Groups like our family provide for our needs and wants, which reduces uncertainty until we can take care of ourselves. When we tell others we are a member of a group, it creates a perception of who we are in their mind.

Uncertainty is reduced between individuals that belong to the same group even if they do not know one another. As a member of the same group they share a common experience, tradition, and understanding of what it means to be a group member. In order to become a member, they may have had to fulfill some requirements or have some specific skills. This can provide information to help reduce uncertainty about them even if we do not know them personally.

We like to be around people who like us and who are like us. We feel safer with others who we perceive to be similar because it reduces uncertainty. This motivates us to join groups so we can learn more about others making them more predictable. When we choose to join a group, it is often based on what types of behavioral norms we find amenable.

We have a natural tendency to join groups when we perceive the others as being similar to us because we share a connection or common bond. We are motivated to join groups with others we find attractive. This can include physical attractiveness, but also other attributes that we find attractive such as likable, knowledgeable, humorous, entertaining, or supportive.

While reducing uncertainty is an important function of groups, having some uncertainty can be good. Groups need some degree of uncertainty to function effectively. When groups reduce uncertainty too much, they might stop looking for new information and generating new ideas because they no longer feel that they have to do so. This creates the perception of confidence that can easily become arrogance, so group members might filter out important information or resist change.

Having some degree of uncertainty can be good for groups, just as it can be helpful for individuals because it makes us think more about new ideas, question our assumptions, challenge what we know, and helps to bring in new ideas so we can look at what we know in a new or different way.

In groups we share our ideas and experiences with others and they share theirs with us. This process of shared meaning gives them greater significance. This is how we convey shared meaning about ourselves to others. When we tell others that we are a member of a particular group, it communicates information about who we are without having to explain everything in detail.

Members participate in rituals and traditions that serve to share meaning about the group. Members communicate with one another what it means to belong to the group. Over time these stories create a group culture and many groups together can create social reality.

Through the process of communicating, groups can have a significant affect on our self-concept by providing us with reflected feedback. We utilize this reflective feedback through the process of communicating to see ourselves as others see us. When we receive positive feedback it can bolster our self-concept.

This motivates us to join groups where we will receive positive feedback that validates our perception of ourselves whether it is accurate or not. When our self-concept is validated it makes us feel valued as a person. This is why we can be reluctant to leave some groups even though the group may not be effective or a positive influence.

Sharing meaning can make us feel an important part of a group, we feel valued and appreciated as an individual. When others accept us it bolsters our self-concept and increases our confidence. Groups can give us a feeling of contributing to others and making a difference. When we help others we can feel good about ourselves.

Some groups are organized to support a cause, to help others, or to make people's lives better. In these cases, the act of helping others can be the reward. It can give people a sense of meaning or purpose in life, a feeling of doing something worthwhile, or being a good person.

As a member of a group, when we need information or help to make decisions or solve a problem, we do not have to figure everything out for ourselves. Instead, we can seek out the help and advice of other members who might have done this before to make us more proficient sooner than we could on our own.

Because of the law of shared meaning we can understand and learn about things from the knowledge and experience of others without necessarily having to do all the work ourselves. As a member of a group we can seek out advice from other members who have had similar experiences to find out what worked for them to help us determine what we should do.

We join groups because the world is a big place and groups help to make it smaller. They help us make sense of our experiences and the world around us to make life more meaningful. When others share their point of view or insight, we can see things in a new way that can help make our experiences more useful to us. Groups provide meaning to our experiences by developing a culture that explains why things are the way they are. They share meaning through rituals and traditions that make life meaningful because we have a connection to others and the past.

Groups and organizations provide an important means of implementing the law of investing. In relationships, we invest in the other person on an individual basis, so if the relationship ends, so do the benefits. Groups and organizations provide a mechanism that allows us to invest in other people on a wholesale basis, even people we do not know.

When one person leaves the group our relationship with the group or the other members does not have to end. This gives us expectations of receiving future benefits for our contributions to the group because groups transcend dependence on individual members. This increases our expectations of stability and predictability about the future.

Groups can provide monetary and material rewards. We invest our time, energy, and other resources in the group and each other in order to fulfill mutual needs and wants. Investments are regulated by the group's rules and norms, which determine how resources are allocated to its members.

As a member of a group, we make connections with many people providing a means to invest in many relationships instead of getting to know only one person at a time. We are motivated to do this because our contribution to the group may be little more than we would contribute to an individual relationship, however, because there are many people in the group we can potentially receive more benefits and rewards. This saves time by not having to get to know every person individually like we do when we form relationships.

Being a member of a group shapes our perceptions of ourselves and others based upon how others communicate with us. It also shapes our perceptions of others outside the group because we make assumptions based upon their group affiliations. Many times when we are part of a group we are expected to look, act, speak, and behave in certain ways to fulfill group norms and rules. We all have perceptions and expectations about ourselves and others. These include what we think we are expected to do for others and what we expect others to do for us. Groups necessitate mutual contributions to achieve common goals by putting the group's interests ahead of the individual.

We have expectations about our experiences in the groups we belong to and perceptions about how those expectations are being met. Tension and conflict can arise when our perceptions do not meet our expectations. In order to avoid misunderstandings, it can be helpful for group members to communicate their perceptions of how those expectations are being met, so that they understand them better.

When everyone has an understanding of what is expected of them and what they can expect from others, the group can avoid unnecessary dissatisfaction that can lead to tension and conflict. When we are part of a group we might assume that the other members think like we do, but the reality is they may not. Since everyone is different, all members of a group contribute differently leading to the perception that some people are doing more work than others, which can lead to tension and conflict in the group.

By regulating member's behavior, groups help create a basis for the norms that comprise their social reality. Groups are a means of socialization. It is through groups that we learn about ourselves, others, and the world around us. We learn about society by participating in our family, school, church, and community. It is in groups that we learn the patterns of communicating and the rules of behavior.

Groups can motivate members to conform to the expectations of the other members of the group because if we behave within the accepted norm, we are more likely to be rewarded. If we behave outside the accepted norm we can be punished. Members who consistently behave outside group norms can be excluded or removed from the group and prohibited from receiving its benefits.

The bank.

We join and stay a member of groups because they allocate resources that fulfill many of our needs and wants. So, when we join a group it could be thought of like joining a cooperative or being approved for a loan by a bank. When we join a group, we can benefit from the resources it has to offer, but first we have to be approved by the members. This motivates us to seek their approval by reducing uncertainty about ourselves, so that the bank will accept us as a member.

The bank is governed by the laws of uncertainty, shared meaning, and investing. When uncertainty about us is reduced, it helps other group members to feel comfortable sharing their resources to invest in us, like having a line of credit to draw on. If the bank does not approve of us, other members may be less likely to share their resources because investment in us has higher uncertainty.

When you become a member of the bank you agree to follow its rules. This includes the patterns of communicating and rules of behavior that have been determined as acceptable for its members. When members follow the rules, uncertainty is reduced and they are perceived as more stable making others more confident investing in them and in the group.

By following the rules we show that we are willing to make a commitment to the group and are worthy of receiving its benefits. Rules help to keep the group together because without them the group would break down into chaos. This exerts some control over the members so that they are more stable now and more predictable in the future.

If we do not follow the rules, we can be perceived as less stable and uncertainty is increased. The group may exert punishments for infractions of the rules to keep its members in line. The bank has to do this because if it doesn't, then there's no reason for anyone to follow the rules and it will fall apart. If infractions continue, we may be shut out or asked to leave the group. This can motivate the group and its members to withdraw their investments in us, so that we no longer benefit from the resources of the bank, in effect closing our line of credit.

If we leave the bank by quitting the group, we are no longer bound by the rules. So, we may be perceived as more uncertain and will not continue to receive its benefits. This is why people can be motivated to stay in groups that they are not happy with or that they do not agree with because they do not want to lose the benefits they receive from them.

When individual members of a group invest in the group and the other members, they are also investing in themselves. This is because when they help the group and the other group members individually, it benefits the group, which in turn benefits them. When the group does well and is successful it can make the other members successful. People are motivated to help one another as part of a group because they have a shared destiny or desired outcome.

When the members of a bank do well, then the bank prospers. When the bank prospers, individual members are likely to do so as well. Conversely, if they are reluctant to help one another or invest in other members, the group may not receive the resources it needs which can undermine its success and its members.

Groups and their members often have connections to other groups and individuals. A group may have the added benefit of allowing its members access to the resources of other groups and organizations, and their members. If a member of one group is approved and in good standing, they may also benefit from the resources of another group. For instance, if the group is part of a larger organization, like a department of a company, resources may be available to all the departments within the organization.

You may have had the experience of leaving a group where you considered the other members to be your friends. After you left, you may have found that you now had little or no contact with the other members. They may no longer contact you or even return phone calls or emails, leaving you wondering what happened. Even if there was some contact after you left, they eventually drifted away over time. This happens because the connection that created the relationship no longer exists. It will fade away unless there is another connection to sustain it.

When a person ceases to be a member of the bank, such as if they quit or are removed, they are no longer permitted the full benefits of the bank. If they were allowed to keep them there would be no reason to join the bank or follow its rules in the first place.

Since change can happen through information coming from outside of the group, maintaining connections with former group members may bring unwanted change to the group threatening its stability. When someone is no longer a member they have less in common with the group. There is likely to be less proximity, familiarity, intensity, or similarity to sustain a connection.

Since most of the communicating at the bank is about bank business, they may no longer have much to communicate about. People have many demands on their limited time, so when someone is no longer a member they no longer have the same connection and other members are less likely to have as much time for them.

Group needs.

We have many needs and wants we cannot fulfill ourselves that can be fulfilled as a member of a group. Groups are attractive because they have the resources and ability to fulfill many of our needs and wants. Groups save us time and effort by fulfilling some of our needs on a continuous basis.

Without groups, every time we had a need or want to be fulfilled we would have to find a way to do so. For example, we work with a group of people in order to provide a regular paycheck to fulfill our monetary needs. If we did not belong to a group by having a job, every time we needed money we would spend time and energy looking for something to do to make it.

Groups can accomplish more to fulfill mutual needs and wants by working together than individuals can by working alone. Groups are able to mobilize resources for their members. They provide for material needs like a salary. We can learn how to do things by benefiting from the expertise and experience of others.

When more people are involved in problem solving there's a greater wealth of knowledge, experience, and expertise. Groups have the potential to make better decisions, solve complex problems, and provide the resources needed to get things done.

Groups fulfill individual needs like our need for affiliation by being around other people. They fulfill our need for inclusion because we have connections with others who consider us a part of the group. They fulfill our need for friendship with other people, so we can trust and confide in them. They fulfill our need for closeness by having others who we care about and who care about our well being. We often form our closest and longest lasting relationships with others who belong to the same groups as we do.

Groups are able to convey many kinds of social rewards that fulfill its members' needs. Groups can fulfill our need for prestige, esteem, and status in ways that we cannot fulfill as individuals. Not all groups are the same, we invest groups with meaning depending upon what they do and who belongs to them. Different groups are perceived differently giving them different levels of status and prestige.

For instance, a professional sports team can have a higher status than an amateur team. When someone joins a group the status of the group is often transferred to the individual member. Alternatively, if a high status person joins the group, the status of that person can be conferred upon all members of the group. When a sports team signs a high profile player it can raise the status of the team and the other members. Some people join groups because of the status or prestige conveyed by the group upon its members.

The process of transference can work for prestige, respect, and self-esteem. If a group is respected or members held in high esteem, their status can transfer to other members of the group. If a member of the group does well, they may be held in high esteem and respected by other members. This process can also work in reverse, if the group develops a bad reputation it can transfer the lack of status or prestige to its members whether they deserve it or not.

Groups give their members the chance to contribute, to feel like they are making a difference, to do something worthwhile, and to develop their talents. Groups often have a hierarchy within the group where members have different ranks or levels of importance. This motivates the members to work for the good of the group so that they can improve their status or rank within the group. The ability to meet needs and wants makes some groups more attractive or powerful than others.

Groups can experience tensions from conflicting needs, wants, and desired outcomes, just as we experience tension as individuals. As individuals, we have tensions between conflicting and competing needs and wants, such as the need for change and stability. Groups can also experience tension between conflicting needs like the need for structure and flexibility. Individual members can experience tension between one another based on their own individual needs and wants.

For instance, members need to spend time working with the group to accomplish group tasks, but they also need to spend time by themselves away from the group with friends and family. Members may be unaware of these tensions and think there is something wrong with them or the others, which can lead unnecessary conflict. In order to be part of an effective group it is helpful to be aware that these tensions exist to mitigate their effect.

Whether the purpose of a group is task or social, groups have tasks that must be accomplished by its members in order for the group to function. This means that members give up some of their autonomy by allowing the group to make some decisions for them in order to gain benefits the group can give in return.

Getting things done is one of the primary reasons we form groups. If a group is not accomplishing its tasks, group members will become dissatisfied with the group creating tension. Even groups that are social in nature have tasks that need to be accomplished such as organizing activities or making a budget.

By participating in social activities we get to know other group members through the process of self-disclosure, which includes telling stories about ourselves and our experiences. We get to know each other by participating in traditions and rituals like celebrating important dates and events. It is through these activities that we get to know others as individuals as well as to reduce stress and just have fun. This is why it's important to socialize in groups by doing things like getting together for coffee or spending time together not doing tasks.

When we get to know others on a more personal social level, we reduce uncertainty, share meanings with them, and develop trust so we can invest in more effective relationships to better carry out the purpose of the group. Without having the social needs of the group met, people can become burned out or dissatisfied with the group leading to tension and conflict reducing their commitment and perhaps motivating them to leave the group.

Every group has to find its own balance between fulfilling task and social needs, but both of these must be addressed for a group to be effective. Some time should be set aside for each because they both cannot be fulfilled simultaneously. This can create a natural tension between the task and social needs of a group.

There is no one right way to fulfill these needs. Each group needs to find the way that works best for them. Some ways to do this can include scheduling time before and after meetings when members can socialize and talk informally with one another. The group can celebrate rituals and traditions. They can spend time together in activities when they do not have to be concerned about accomplishing a task.

How Groups Are Formed

Groups are formed by making connections with others and communicating through those connections. In order to form groups we must first make a connection with others. To do this we have to meet them for the first time.

In order to be part of a group, we have to make a connection with others so that we can meet them. Since we are only able to come in contact with a finite number of people, we have limited options of what groups we can join.

So, we often rely on familiar patterns of communicating that follow the rules of social reality. People create groups for reasons that can be as varied as the individuals who create them. We are motivated to create groups to help us fulfill mutual needs and wants that we cannot fulfill ourselves. The advantage of joining a group is that they can fulfill needs and wants on an ongoing basis rather than negotiating with others every time we need something.

In groups we get to know many people over long periods of time reducing uncertainty increasing predictability and stability. Groups help us to communicate with others by making connections with them. Groups help make life more meaningful by sharing our experiences with others. Groups can provide structure and future predictability enabling us to invest resources in others to achieve mutual desired outcomes. They increase security, stability, and predictability motivating us to form groups in practically all areas of our lives.

A group's identity is not so much about the individual members, but rather the relationships members create collectively with one another. This is why people can act one way in one group and a different way in another group. If members act as individuals, there is not much of a group identity. In order for them to be a group, there has to be connections and some degree of coordination between them. In order to do this, each person must give up something in order to gain something in return.

In relationships, two people communicate directly with one another negotiating everything between themselves creating a balance of power. Groups have a different climate because by adding a third person the balance of power shifts, changing the nature of how they communicate with one another. Each person now divides their attention between the other two. Chances are each person communicates more with one person than the other creating an imbalance.

Since we contribute resources and receive benefits in relationships, adding a third person can change the nature of how they are distributed. With three people there is the potential for two of them to make decisions giving them power over the third person. You have likely experienced a relationship with a friend who then got a new friend, girlfriend or boyfriend, or perhaps got married. Chances are the nature of your relationship and how you communicated with them changed.

Groups usually have more than three people, but when we go from a two person relationship to three people or a larger group, how they communicate with one another changes. There will be people who communicate more with some and less with others. How resources are distributed can create an imbalance in the group.

Group Development

All groups have one thing in common, at one time the group's members did not know each other. This means that all groups go through the process of group development. This process can be characterized by four phases that are governed by the laws of uncertainty, shared meaning, and investing. Since every group is different there is no one right way to develop a group.

A group can go through these phases rather quickly or they might take some time. How a group goes through these phases depends on the nature of the group, the individuals involved, and the group's needs, wants, and desired outcomes.

1. Group creation, the law of uncertainty phase. Individuals come together to form a group motivated by individual needs and wants in order to achieve mutual desired outcomes. They may know little or nothing about one another, so they need to reduce uncertainty to function as a group.

2. Group growth, the law of shared meaning phase. Once uncertainty has been reduced to a level that members are comfortable with, they share meaning to develop their social reality, which includes the group's structure, boundaries, norms, roles, and rules of behavior.

3. Group maintenance, the law of investing phase. Once group members know more about the group, they begin to feel comfortable investing their time, energy, and other resources in the group and in one another in order to work together to achieve their desired outcomes.

4. Group dissolution, return to the law of uncertainty phase. There are times when a group no longer functions and may cease to exist increasing uncertainty.

I. Group Creation, The Law of Uncertainty Phase

The first phase of group development is motivated by the law of uncertainty. People are first drawn together based upon the connections they have with one another. People form groups for many of the same reasons they form relationships. They may be in close proximity, share common interests, or have similar desired outcomes. They are motivated to do this in order to reduce uncertainty, so that they can fulfill needs and wants they cannot fulfill as individuals.

Every group has one thing in common, at one time it did not exist. Every group member has one thing in common, at one time they did not belong to the group. Every group had to be created and every group member has to go through the process of joining the group. Even if a person was part of forming a group, they still go through the process that new members go through to get accustomed to the group and its members.

When we meet with a group for the first time we want to make a good impression. We use identity management to shape the impressions others have of us by presenting ourselves as we want them to perceive us. We want to be perceived as likable, so they will like us because we like being liked. We want to be perceived as agreeable, so they will get along with us. We want to be perceived as being helpful, so they will help us. We want to be supportive of others, so they will support us. We do this because we want to be perceived as someone who would be a good group member.

We want to make a good impression, so when we first get to know someone we reduce uncertainty by following the rules of social reality. We make a good impression by how we communicate, both verbally and nonverbally. We talk about general subjects to get things started while looking for specific topics that might be interesting to talk about. We use conversational skills to create a natural flow being careful not to talk too much or too little. We utilize positive nonverbal body language such as smiling, facial expressions, and eye contact to make a connection.

In order to reduce uncertainty, we utilize information that is available to us when we first meet someone to develop a first impression. Since we don't know the others we probably have little information about them, so we form an impression based on the information that's available, such as what they say and how they use nonverbal body language. If there is information missing, we fill in the gaps using our past experiences whether it is accurate or not.

When meeting new people we often have a heightened sense of self-awareness giving us a feeling of apprehension or anxiety. Anxiety is an emotional feeling based upon increased uncertainty. We might focus on how we are coming across to others because we want to make a good impression so they will like us.

This may create feelings of uncertainty or awkwardness in the conversation because we are searching for common ground as well as trying to determine how others perceive us. We don't usually consider that the others may also be just as concerned about how they are coming across to us. When we feel anxiety we are more likely to communicate on a superficial level.

This level of communicating cannot continue for very long because if there is too much uncertainty, people will not be able to get things done. This means that one of the first tasks a group faces is the challenge of reducing uncertainty in order to decrease individual apprehension so that they can function as a group.

This can be done through conversation with appropriate self-disclosure, so that members can find common ground to reduce uncertainty enough to begin to function as a group. When they feel more comfortable with one another, they are better able to communicate in more depth and build common connections enabling them to get to know one another better.

Whenever we join a group we can find ourselves in an unfamiliar situation motivating us to look for ways to communicate with others. If we are not sure what to do, we may fall back on past experience, which may or may not help. If uncertainty is too high, we may hold back and not talk very much letting others do all the talking, which can make us feel like an outsider.

In these circumstances it can be helpful to use familiar patterns of communicating that are part of the rules of social reality. Patterns of communicating are predetermined methods of interacting with others that work like a script in a play or movie. They help to reduce uncertainty because we have heard them before. We use them because learning how to communicate in every situation we face would be difficult and time consuming.

We use patterns of communicating to reduce uncertainty in many common situations such as a job interview, first date, going to the grocery store, or meeting people we don't know. These patterns include simple greetings as well as more complex ways of interacting. They tell us what we should say and do to act properly in a given situation.

For example, a common pattern of communicating when we meet someone is to say, "Hello, how are you?" And the expected reply is, "Good, thank you." We are not supposed to actually tell them how we feel. If we did, it would be unexpected and not part of the established patterns of communicating, so they may not know how to respond.

We use familiar patterns of communicating when we first form a group to get things going until the group members get to know each other well enough to develop their own ways of communicating. They may rely on their past experiences in other groups and behave in ways that they have done in the past regardless of the new situation. This can create a feeling of stiffness and awkwardness within the group because everyone is uncertain how to communicate with one another.

Some people may hold back by not participating and letting others dominate the conversation. While patterns of communicating work initially, a group cannot effectively accomplish its tasks or achieve its desired outcome in this manner. The group needs to develop its own method of communicating between members. By knowing how this process works, you can help a group to become more effective.

Balancing the Group

A group is only as effective as the individuals that comprise it. This makes the choice of who is in a group important to its success. Some groups develop naturally and members have little or no choice over who is in the group. Some groups are open to anyone who wants to join. Some groups are purposely created to achieve specific desired outcomes so there may be criteria that determines who can join.

Other groups place restrictions or requirements on who they allow in the group in order to maintain a perception of exclusivity or the professionalism of the group. They may have requirements like earning a degree or passing a test to maintain professional standards and public confidence in the group.

Choosing group members may be the single most important task facing any group. To create a group that works well together takes balance. Balancing a group involves balancing the roles people play within the group. It is finding the right combination of experience, skills, and expertise relevant to the task. It takes the right combination of communicating skills. For example, a group made up of all leaders may have a more difficult time working together than one that is more balanced with people who have experience in more supportive roles.

In choosing members for a group consider what they bring to the group. While it is important to give consideration to their expertise and work skills, they also bring with them their communicating skills, behavior, attitudes, and past experiences. Consideration should be given to their social skills and ability to work with others. People may be good at what they do, but they might have difficulty working in a group with others.

II. Group Growth, The Law of Shared Meaning Phase

When a group first comes together there is a high degree of uncertainty because people are unsure what to say and how to act creating an atmosphere of awkwardness and formality. Once group members get to know one another, they reduce uncertainty to a level of comfort that enables them to work together so the group can grow and develop.

When members are comfortable with one another, they begin to talk about themselves and their past experiences. They share stories about themselves, others, and the group. This begins the law of shared meaning phase of group development. Sharing meaning helps to create a common understanding within the group of what the group means and what it means to be a member.

A group has meaning to both its members and those outside the group. A group can be like an individual person, it can develop a unique identity separate from the individuals that comprise it. Members may express that identity by giving their group a name and symbols like a logo, mascot, or group colors. If the group has been given a name by outsiders, like in a company or department, the members may put their own mark on it like giving it a nickname.

Sharing meaning lets members know what the group stands for and what it means to be a member. This is communicated through the stories members tell and their history, traditions, and rituals. Groups can utilize identity management, much as individuals do, to manage what they communicate about themselves with people outside the group that affects their perceptions and achieve their desired outcomes.

Groups, like individuals, have needs and wants that must be fulfilled to achieve their desired outcomes so the group can function. This motivates individual members to take action to accomplish them. Groups have many members to accomplish these tasks, but everyone cannot do the same thing at the same time. This means that group members need to specialize by taking on specific tasks, roles, and responsibilities.

Since there are many people doing many tasks, groups need structure in order to coordinate their activities. If everyone did whatever they wanted, the group would become chaotic and nothing would get done.

Developing a group structure includes creating rules and standard operating procedures which members accept as their normal means of behavior, commonly called norms. In naturally occurring groups, norms are often not predetermined, so the members will have to create them as they go.

In groups that are intentionally created, like in a business, the structure may be established in advance, but the members may still need to negotiate how they will get things done. The law of shared meaning helps group members function effectively. Two ways groups do this is using the process of behavioral reinforcement and self-disclosure.

Self-disclosure.

Self-disclosure encourages investing in groups much like it does in relationships. It is a means by which we make connections with one another. Group members talk about themselves and about their past experiences. Members take turns contributing to the collective experience of the group.

Disclosure begins at a very superficial level by talking about commonly known information such as where people live, what they do for a living, and recent events. As people share information they become more comfortable sharing more personal information. As group members get to know one another it reduces uncertainty so that they are more familiar and predictable enabling them to trust each other to contribute their resources to work together.

Self-disclosure is more effective when we share information as we feel comfortable and when we feel it's appropriate. Disclosure should be reciprocated so everyone feels like they are contributing fairly to the group. This way no one feels they are contributing more information about themselves than anyone else.

Too much disclosure, shared too fast can be considered inappropriate potentially scaring people away. Too little disclosure can be perceived as holding back, being evasive, or being aloof. Individual members can utilize feedback to determine the appropriate level of self-disclosure that itself may become a group norm.
Behavioral reinforcement in groups.

Groups develop their own specialized ways of communicating and doing things through the process of behavioral reinforcement. This process begins by using familiar patterns of communicating as members exhibit behaviors to accomplish tasks based upon their past experience and perceptions.

The group selects which behaviors it deems appropriate for the group and seeks to eliminate those it does not. To do this, members may utilize the process of communicating to share their Great Idea with others in the group and then wait for feedback. The nature of the feedback they receive at this early stage can determine the future behavior of the group.

When group members communicate or exhibit a behavior, it is accepted, rejected, or met with ambivalence by the other members. If the other members accept it, it can become part of the group's norms, roles, or rules.

If it is rejected, it will not be a part of the group culture, and if the response is not clear, it may be repeated until it gets a response. Behavioral reinforcement is an important process to be aware of because it affects how a group communicates and behaves, which can determine its effectiveness resulting in success or failure.

Group norms.

The process of behavioral reinforcement creates a set of normal standard operating procedures, called norms. Groups do this because the members have to work together to develop their own ways of doing things. Norms consist of just about anything that is considered normal for the group.

Norms refer to a group's normal pattern of behavior consisting of the shared expectations that members have for behavior in the group. They let members know what is expected of them and what they can expect from the others. They often include how group members communicate with one another, how they behave, and how they make decisions, solve problems, and resolve conflicts.

The way that group members first accomplish a task can set a precedent, which if repeated can establish a norm as part of their standard operating procedures.

For example, how the group resolves their first conflict may be repeated when conflicts reoccur whether it was effective or not. Precedents work rather like first impressions. They may not be effective, but after they have been established, they can be difficult to change.

This is a process that happens naturally or it can be purposely managed. Precedents may be created haphazardly that can hinder the group's success making it difficult to change later on. It can be helpful to be aware of how this process works in order to develop precedents early in the group's history that create positive norms to help the group achieve its desired outcomes.

In order to form a fully functioning group, norms need to be stabilized so that group members will share the same perceptions and expectations. They need to know what is expected of them and what they can expect from the other members.

People don't like surprises or uncertainty, they want stability and predictability especially in others who are close to them and with whom they share a common purpose. Without norms every group member would do whatever they felt like doing reducing the group to chaos so nothing would get done. Norms provide a means of establishing boundaries for behavior and structure so the group can accomplish its tasks.

Group roles.

Norms are the shared expectations that group members have of the group's behavior and roles are the shared expectations members have of each individual member. Groups have needs and wants that must be fulfilled, desired outcomes to be met, and tasks to be accomplished. In order to accomplish them, someone has to do the work and who does what work comprises a role. A role is a specialized type of behavioral norm consisting of the perceptions and expectations that each member has about their responsibilities in the group.

Roles are based on the needs and wants of the group because this is how they are fulfilled. A role in the group is rather like a role of an actor in a play or movie. Each actor knows what they and the other actors are going to do providing predictability enabling them to perform their role. Roles let group members know who is responsible for doing what tasks, so that each person can do their job and the group can function effectively.

Roles in groups can be developed through the process of behavioral reinforcement similar to how norms are established. Groups need to have things done and group members need to do them. Group members take on individual tasks and their actions are either accepted, rejected, or met with indifference by the other members. When the group approves of what a member does the member will fill a role and when everyone has their role, the group's structure will stabilize.

If the group responds negatively or ignores a member's behavior their role will not be established because it is not supported. It's helpful to have an awareness of how this process works to help stabilize roles, norms, and rules within the group as soon as feasible, so it can function effectively and get on to accomplishing its tasks.

Norms and roles develop because a group has to establish certain behaviors and ways of communicating in order to fulfill its needs and wants, so it can accomplish its tasks. If everyone does whatever they want or if they all do the same thing, then the group will be in disarray increasing uncertainty.

Since the law of uncertainty motivates people to take action to reduce uncertainty because it's uncomfortable, group members will be motivated to reduce it by developing group norms and roles. The group has to reduce uncertainty in order to work effectively, so it can accomplish its tasks. How it does this is usually governed by a set of rules so everyone knows what to expect.

Group rules.

In order for groups to function properly, there needs to be a mechanism to regulate behavior. That mechanism helps to establish the rules for the group. Where norms are shared expectations of group behavior and roles are shared expectations of individual behavior, rules are the shared expectations of how both are governed. Rules gives the people who make them power over the behavior of the other group members. Rules can be negotiated between group members over time or established when it first forms.

When a group first forms it may have no rules, so members look for guidance from the rules of social reality. A group may utilize rules from its members, other groups, or from a larger organization if it is part of one. Even if the rules are established when the group first forms, there is often an informal process by which the unwritten rules are established.

Rules are often created by the process of behavioral reinforcement, so members exhibit different behaviors that are either accepted or rejected by the other group members. Members try out different behaviors based upon their past experience and their perceptions of the needs and wants of the group. When a behavior is deemed acceptable by group members and is repeated over time, it can become part of the norms of the group.

Rules are necessary in order to reduce uncertainty, create stability, and increase predictability so that group members can invest their resources in one another and in the group. Without rules no one would know what to do or how to behave and the group could not function.

Group structure.

Groups need structure because it creates stability to reduce uncertainty. This provides predictability so that people can invest in the group and work together to accomplish its tasks. Structure is necessary for many aspects of the group including its roles, rules, norms, networks, and boundaries. Smaller groups generally have less structure since everyone can communicate directly with everyone else. As groups grow in size, communicating between members becomes more difficult, so more structure is needed for it to function effectively.

Group structure benefits both members and those outside the group by helping them to better understand how it works. How a group is structured can communicate confidence, competence, responsibility, and professionalism to others. This helps group members accomplish their tasks by understanding the group and its purpose. Structure helps members understand how they fit into the group and how what they do contributes to the benefit of everyone.

Having a formally recognized structure gives groups legitimacy by letting outsiders know who is responsible for what tasks. As a group becomes more structured, it may have more formal positions as part of its structure like president, CEO, secretary, or treasurer. These positions give the group legitimacy and creates the perception of professionalism and competence.

Groups not only have formal structure they also have informal structure. A formal structure is comprised of the ways in which group members are expected to interact with one another. This structure may not have been created by the group members themselves, but by other people outside the group such as a larger organization.

The informal structure often reflects how members actually communicate and their everyday behavior. As organizations become larger they need to develop structures to function effectively, but these can also serve as barriers to effective communicating. This can motivate members to utilize informal networks by making connections that get around bureaucratic rules so that they can get things done.

Group networks.

Networks are a series of connections between people that transfers information in, out, and around a group. Groups often utilize strategies in the form of norms to manage their boundaries to maintain their group's integrity rather like countries use borders and customs to control what goes in and out of a country.

In a group, not every member talks with every other member the same amount or in the same manner. A network consists of who communicates with whom, under what circumstances, and about what information. Networks help to fulfill group members need for information. How information flows in and out of the group can tell a lot about the group, its openness, its rules, its boundaries, and its structure.

Formal networks follow an established hierarchy carrying official information for the group or organization. Informal networks generally carry information that people are interested in and want to receive. Networks work because they follow the process of communicating by making connections between people.

One member can serve as a liaison or gatekeeper to bring information into the group or keep information out. The more connected a member is to other networks, the more information they are likely to have access to, which can give them more power within the group.

III. Group Maintenance, The Law of Investing Phase

Once uncertainty has been reduced and group members share meaning to develop the group, they need to invest in the group and each other to maintain the group. Groups provide benefits, but they also require contributions from their members. These contributions can be in the form of time, energy, emotions, attention, and material things like money.

The perceptions and expectations members have of receiving benefits for contributions can affect their satisfaction with their group, their commitment to the group, and what they are willing to do for the group. This begins the law of investing phase of group development, which is necessary to maintain the group over time.

When a group stabilizes, uncertainty is reduced making it more predictable. This gives the group a greater chance of having longevity, which creates value because it motivates members to stay with the group longer to receive benefits. When people have a perception of receiving future benefits from the group, it gives them a reasonable expectation that they will see the investment they make now payoff in the future.

Individual members invest in the group when they begin to identify with the group and see it as their own. They may refer to the group as "my group" or "our group." This is an expression of their collective sense of ownership and pride in the group. When they introduce themselves to others outside the group, they may mention that they are members of the group. They may even define their self-concept and manage their identity based upon belonging to the group.

Group satisfaction.

Satisfaction represents the degree to which an individual member is happy with the group based upon their perceptions and expectations. It is often based upon how well they feel their expectations have been met and the extent to which their needs and wants have been fulfilled. The more members feel that these are being met, the greater their satisfaction increasing their commitment to the group. They are likely to do more for the group because they will not want to lose their benefits.

Group satisfaction is often based on the perceptions and expectations of individual members. Everyone has expectations of what they want to contribute as well as receive from the groups they join. Most people expect to make fair contributions and receive fair rewards. These perceptions are usually based upon a person's past experiences and what they have received in the past. For instance, what some may consider generous monetary compensation, others may see as inadequate.

Group satisfaction is often based upon the degree to which members feel their needs and wants are being fulfilled by the group. We join groups to fulfill needs and wants we cannot fulfill ourselves, which creates expectations about what we feel we should receive as a member of the group. When a member's perception matches or exceeds their expectations, it can increase their satisfaction with the group.

So, if members have the perception that their needs and wants are being reasonably fulfilled, they are more likely to contribute to the group increasing their satisfaction with the group. After all, if group members are getting their needs and wants fulfilled, why would they want to leave?

If group members feel that their needs and wants are not being fulfilled, they may be less likely to feel satisfaction with the group. If their perceptions are not meeting their expectations, it can motivate them to look at other groups to see if they can do better. This can create dissatisfaction eroding their commitment to the group. If they become dissatisfied enough they might leave the group.

Each member's investment is based upon their perceptions and expectations. Members are likely to have perceptions of the group and what is expected of them, so they are willing to contribute based upon their expectation of future benefits.

Contrary to popular belief, people don't usually seek to maximize rewards and minimize costs by buying low and selling high. Rather, they seek fair rewards for fair contributions. This is because no one wants to be in a group with someone who does as little as possible and expects to get as much as possible.

It can be helpful for groups to be aware of how people outside the group can influence their effectiveness. This is because group members don't get all their support such as their needs and wants fulfilled by the group itself. They often depend on people outside the group to fulfill them, which can give these people some degree of influence in the group.

The support members get from their families can help improve their self-concept and feeling of satisfaction raising their collective self-esteem within the group. A group may have social events that include these people in order to keep them informed about the group and to learn more about their perceptions and expectations.

It can be helpful to be aware of the degree to which group members are satisfied with the group. All too often member dissatisfaction goes unnoticed, ignored, or members keep it to themselves because they don't want to be characterized as a complainer or risk their investment.

Members who tell others that they are dissatisfied with the group may be punished by the other members to discourage dissent from spreading throughout the group. If members feel they could lose their investment, they could withhold their problems with the group until it builds up to the point where they can no longer deal with the tension, creating conflict or they may quit.

Dissatisfaction can be reduced by encouraging group members to share their thoughts and feelings without the fear of retaliation. Groups may not be in a position to offer more material rewards, however, it is relatively easy to offer social rewards such as acknowledgment, recognition, and respect to bolster members' self-concept. Utilizing these methods is effective because agreement is one of the strongest means of supporting others and it affirms their value to the group. When our ideas are accepted by others it elevates our status with the group.

Group commitment.

Commitment is the degree to which individual group members are attracted to be a member of the group. It is the degree to which they put group goals above their own. It is the degree to which they are willing to stay with the group through difficult times and to resolve conflicts. It is the degree to which they are willing to work hard to complete a task without regard to gaining personal rewards. Commitment can be a measure of how strong the connections are between individual group members.

A member's commitment can be seen as a measure of their investment in the group and in the other members. Commitment is based upon an individual's perception and expectation of their needs and wants being fulfilled by the group in the short and long term. Investments come in different forms depending upon an individual's needs. Some members may forgo short term rewards with the expectation of greater long term rewards such as working for a higher purpose or a retirement pension.

Group power.

Groups are attractive because they concentrate power and people want the benefits that power can bring. Power can provide a means to fulfill many of our needs and wants. When people are grouped together they create hierarchies, ranks, or a kind of pecking order among members, which gives some of them power over others.

Power based hierarchies are often expressed by the amount of respect, status, and prestige that is given to fulfill the needs of its members. Groups concentrate power because they are comprised of people who gather and allocate resources, which means that someone has to decide who gets what. Because members have needs and wants they seek to have fulfilled by groups, the people who distribute resources have power over those who want their benefits.

Groups have tasks that need to be accomplished, so people have to do them. Some tasks are more important than others, so they are ranked or prioritized. Some tasks are more difficult, require more education or expertise, or are done by members who have been in the organization the longest. The law of shared meaning invests these tasks with different values, which creates power, ranks, and hierarchies. This is evidenced by the wide range of salaries organizations often pay their employees.

Groups create power because they have the ability to fulfill needs and wants. This motivates members to do what the group wants them to do so they can have them fulfilled. If they want to gain benefits, they have to comply with the rules of the group. Groups create rules that control member's behavior and provide punishments for those who violate them. Groups can do this because they control and distribute resources by determining who receives them and who does not. These resources help members fulfill both social and material needs and wants.

Power is attractive because of its ability to reduce uncertainty by creating safety, security, and predictability. Power is necessary in society for the protection of its citizens to keep them free from harm. It is a way to get the things done that need to be done in order for society to function. Power is attractive because of its ability to allocate resources and benefits. People want to be around others who they perceive as powerful with the expectation that they will be the beneficiary of some of those resources. They have the expectation of power transference, if they are near others who are powerful they may be perceived as having power and status themselves.

We have a tendency to invest power with shared meaning. We look at power as being something that can be a positive force for good as well as a destructive force. Power is based upon things having value and sharing meaning often gives them value, so power is often based upon what meanings people share. People compete for things they consider valuable giving these things power over their behavior. This means that power can be based on the shared meanings we have about things, people, and groups. It can be measured by how much a person is willing to do to get what they want.

Power is based upon our perceptions and expectations. It is based on our perception of the degree to which others have control or influence over us. Power is the manifestation of our expectation of receiving future benefits for present behaviors. It is important in groups because it keeps them together and motivates its members to behave in ways that helps the group function.

Groups can exert power over their members because the members have expectations of receiving benefits that will fulfill their needs and wants. The more people expect to gain, the more likely they are to submit to the power of the group. The degree to which power can be exerted is often the degree to which the group can fulfill their needs and wants.

Group longevity.

One reason we form groups is because they have longevity beyond their individual members. Over time, a group's founders are eventually replaced with new members. As a group grows older, members eventually leave, so it must attract new members to keep it going or the group will cease to exist. This creates a hierarchy within the group giving members who have been there the longest higher status and more power than new members.

Older members often have more experience, more expertise, and more knowledge about the group. They also know the group better, know how it works, and how to get things done. Groups often rank their members in a pecking order from the highest to the least status based in part on how long they have been a member.

Groups provide rewards to their members based upon how long they have been a member of the group. These can be material rewards such as salary and bonuses. They can be tangible rewards like a bigger office with nicer furniture in a more desirable location. They can also be social rewards like respect, status, influence, and power. Groups often allocate rewards based on how long a person has been with the group to provide an incentive to encourage members to invest their time and other resources over long periods of time.

This helps to ensure the continuation of the group after the founders and other members are gone. It helps to increase the attractiveness of the group because members know they can increase the return on their investment by staying longer. This creates stability increasing the potential longevity of the group by motivating people to make contributions now with the expectation of receiving benefits later. This motivates them to make long term investments rather than seek short term rewards, which should benefit the group.

While there are benefits to promoting group longevity it can also lead to group paralysis. When members keep their position in the group for long periods of time it can discourage others from staying in the group or new members from joining.

This is because it could create the perception that the long time members receive all the benefits and resources, so newer members will have to wait a long time before they receive them, if at all. The perception that a few people are receiving most of the benefits may create dissatisfaction, even anger among the other group members. This can lead to stagnation and resistance to innovation, which can be more likely to happen in older organizations.

Group conformity.

Large groups and organizations use power hierarchies to encourage conformity to the group. Members are motivated to make a commitment to the group over long periods of time in order to move up the hierarchy to gain increased rewards. In businesses, this can come in the form of promotions and increased salary. The use of differential power and rewards can work in large organizations, but can undermine the effectiveness of smaller groups.

Groups exert pressure on members to conform to the rules of the group. The more a person wants to be the member of a group, the more willing they may be to change their behavior to belong to it. The degree of pressure to conform is often related to the attractiveness of the group and its ability to fulfill individual needs and wants.

The more a group can fulfill the needs and wants of its members and the more their perceptions meet or exceed expectations, the more attractive the group will be and the more likely members will change their behavior to conform to the group.

Groups have pressures to conform, but they need a mechanism to provide exceptions to conformity to facilitate change. In the larger society, social reality dictates acceptable behavior, however, some people behave outside those rules in order to introduce new ideas or bring about change. For instance, artists, musicians, writers, actors, and celebrities may be allowed to deviate from the norms of society to bring about change such as new styles of clothing, music, art, and new ways of thinking.

This mechanism utilizes the process of behavioral reinforcement. If others find these behaviors acceptable through positive feedback, they may catch on and become more widely adopted. Many types of art and music once considered scandalous are now widely accepted. If there were no such mechanism, society would be less likely to change and could stagnate.

IV. Group Dissolution, Return to The Law of Uncertainty Phase

There's an old saying that goes, all good things come to an end, and many groups come to an end. When people create or join groups they probably never considered how the group will end or that it would ever end at all. Not all groups last forever, eventually many come to an end for a wide variety of reasons.

They may have accomplished their task, they may no longer be fulfilling the needs and wants of their members, or they may no longer be relevant. The group may have lost its founder or members who were the driving force behind the group. Since groups are created for a purpose, the purpose it was created for may no longer exist and the group has simply run its course. In these circumstances the time may have come to disband the group and part ways.

Some groups may realize that their time has come to an end, while others may fight on against the odds. We spend a great deal of time with others in groups, so when it ends we can feel a loss in our lives. However, it may be better to intentionally end a group that has come to the end of the line rather than painfully trying to keep it going as it slowly dwindles away.

Groups have traditions and rituals that celebrate important events for the group and its members. When someone retires there is often a celebration to commemorate their accomplishments. Instead of letting the group slowly wither away, the group members could have this kind of event to retire the group and bring it to a close. The event can be used to celebrate the accomplishments of the group and its members giving them closure by spending one last time together as a group.

Chapter 6
Organizational Communicating

We create organizations because they have the ability to reduce uncertainty in ways that individuals and groups cannot do. They can do this because they have the ability to gather and allocate resources for their members. Organizations can make their members feel safe and secure by reducing uncertainty. They reduce uncertainty by creating structure, so members know what is expected of them and what they can expect of others.

By working together with others, organizations can accomplish tasks that individuals could not accomplish working alone. They have longevity, the ability to continue to exist long after the founders and current members are gone, increasing stability and predictability for their members. They reduce uncertainty by fulfilling material, social, status, and security needs making them attractive to join.

Organizations are held together by the connections between members that form communicating networks through which they share meaning. Members share meaning about the organization including its history, how it was founded, its values, and common purpose. They share meaning about what it means to be a member of the organization. They share meaning about the experiences of the members of the organization through the process of self-disclosure.

This can help to encourage their members to trust one another enough to be able to work together. Members share meaning by participating in traditions and rituals like celebrating important events and special days. An organization's name and logo are invested with meaning telling their members and the public who they are and what they do.

Organizations have structure to provide stability, so that people will be willing to invest their time and other resources in it and in the other members. They utilize boundaries, hierarchies, and levels of authority to create structure that gives the organization and some of its member's power. They develop rules of behavior, so that everyone knows what is expected of them and what they can reasonably expect from others. They allocate resources, provide rewards, and issue punishments to maintain order, so that people will feel comfortable investing in them.

Many aspects of an organization are created and motivated by the law of investing to ensure its stability and longevity, without which people would consider it risky and be unwilling to invest the resources necessary for it to function.

An organization can work like a marketplace where communicating is the currency and people are constantly making offers that are being accepted and rejected.

Understanding organizational behavior and how members communicate with one another can work rather like a balance sheet that can be utilized to analyze the effectiveness of an organization. It can measure how willing people are to invest in it and each other, and how much of a return they expect on their investment.

The difference between an individual's perceptions and expectations can be an indicator of their commitment. The degree to which their needs and wants are being met can be an indicator of their satisfaction or dissatisfaction, which can affect their commitment to the organization.

An organization can be like an individual with its own needs and wants that must be fulfilled in order to function. It exists for a reason and its members must accomplish tasks to achieve its desired outcomes. If they don't, the organization will not function and might cease to exist.

An organization can function like a relationship because it is created by the connections between individuals, so no one person has total control over it. It is a separate entity from the people who comprise it because they create it between them. While members contribute to its existence, it can take on a life of its own with its own personality.

Individual members have their own needs and wants to fulfill, which motivates them to join an organization. Organizations are attractive because they fulfill many needs and wants in ways that individuals cannot. They fulfill not only monetary needs, but also the need for inclusion, status, respect, self-esteem, growth, and a feeling of contributing something worthwhile to make a difference.

Tension can be created between the needs and wants of the organization and the individual members. However, individuals must put the organization's needs first in order for the organization to function effectively.

Organizations create their own specialized version of social reality that serves as a form of social control to regulate individual member's behavior. Members create and share social reality when they tell stories about the organization, its history, important events, and its members. Sometimes these are stories about the early days or overcoming adversity.

An organization often communicates its own social reality including its history, how it was founded, and why it exists, which can include stories about the founders, what kind of people they were, and their achievements.

While these stories are based upon fact, there is often an element of added drama to make them more exciting. These stories are more than just reminiscences of the past, they have a message for members today about the organization. They communicate organizational expectations about its values and how members should behave.

Sharing these stories is motivated by the law of shared meaning because it creates a connection that brings members together for a common purpose. For example, people tell stories about the history of the United States including historical figures like George Washington and Thomas Jefferson. These stories have a message beyond a recollection of events, they communicate a deeper message of communal values and beliefs. They are used to share social reality like what America stands for and what it means to be an American.

Organizational satisfaction.

Everyone has perceptions and expectations about themselves, others, and the organization. They have expectations about what they are supposed to contribute and receive. They have perceptions about how well those expectations are being met, which may or may not reflect reality. Members often have differing perceptions and expectations that can make them feel satisfied or dissatisfied about their role in the organization. Satisfaction helps to increase a member's commitment encouraging them to do their job more effectively. Dissatisfaction can decrease commitment making people unhappy, perhaps even motivating them to leave.

Satisfaction is an emotional response to an individual's perception of the difference between what they are contributing to an organization compared to what they are receiving from it based on their expectations. Everyone's expectations are different because they are based on past experiences, comparisons to others, and their self-concept. When people perceive that they are receiving fair rewards for fair work they are more likely to be satisfied. When they feel they are contributing, but not receiving fair rewards, they can become dissatisfied. This means that member satisfaction is often based upon their perception of how well their needs and wants are being fulfilled, which may or may not reflect reality.

Generally, the higher degree of satisfaction the more an individual is motivated to commit to the organization by contributing their time and resources. The law of investing motivates people to reduce or withdraw their commitment in an organization when they feel they are not getting fair rewards. This is why it can be helpful to understand how member satisfaction works because when members are dissatisfied, it can undermine the effectiveness of the organization. This can reduce their commitment motivating them to withdraw resources and perhaps even leave. While there will always be some dissatisfaction in any organization, if the level becomes too great it may no longer be able to function effectively.

Organizational growth.

Organizations are created much the way groups are created. They can be formed spontaneously out of shared interests or created intentionally to achieve specific desired outcomes. They can grow naturally by people getting together based on their mutual interests that can attract others growing the organization without a clear plan. They can be started by a founder or a group of people to accomplish specific tasks like running a business. An organization often starts out small and when it becomes successful, it attracts other people and grows larger. When an organization gets too large to function as a single group, it will divide into two or more groups creating the need for an organizational structure to keep it together.

When an organization grows so large that everyone cannot communicate directly, like face to face with everyone else, it needs to develop structures so it can function. This increases an organization's needs and wants requiring more people to fulfill them. As an organization grows, the nature of the tasks shift from the original purpose for which it was established to organizing the organization.

For example, a person starts a store that is successful, so it expands to other locations. As it grows, the focus shifts from selling things to managing store locations and employees. Employees are no longer hired just to sell things in the store, but also to run the organization doing managerial tasks such as accounting, human resources, and property management. These tasks must now be accomplished, so the organization can function before anything is actually sold.

Organizational structure.

In order to function effectively, organizations need structure including rules, roles, and norms of behavior. Structure usually consists of different types of connections between members. Organizations need to develop structure so that they can accomplish their tasks and achieve their desired outcomes. Structure can be defined by the boundaries that exist in and around the organization. Organizational structure should be clearly communicated, so all members understand what is expected of them and what they can expect of others, because how an organization structures itself can bring people together or it can divide them by pushing them apart.

Rules are the means by which an organization implements its version of social reality. Most organizations have their own set of both formal and informal rules. The formal rules are often written down in the form of official handbooks, guidelines, contracts, and other written documents. The purpose is to regulate individual behavior by conforming to the norms and expectations of the organization to help it to accomplish its tasks.

New rules are often instituted after there has been some incident or infraction. Rules tend to be more reactive than proactive, often written in response to problems. Rules can be presented in the context that they are there to protect the individual members, however, since they are created by the organization, their purpose is more often to protect the organization.

In addition to the formal organizational rules, groups within the organization often create their own set of informal rules. These rules are rarely written down, but can be more effective in regulating the behavior of its members. They are often created by the members through the process of behavioral reinforcement. Most of the time we only learn about these rules after they have been broken and we are reprimanded. We can learn them by observing the behavior of others or asking a more experienced member.

Organizational networks.

Individuals need information to reduce uncertainty, so they can invest in the organization and in one another in order to work together. In order to fulfill this need, organizations have official networks to disseminate information through connections such as emails, memos, and publications like newsletters. However, this may not be enough to fulfill the need for information. In order to fulfill that need members create connections with others based on similarity, proximity, intensity, and familiarity to form communicating networks which can become a part of an organization's structure.

In many organizations, information tends to flow from the top down, but not so much from the bottom up. People tend to be more comfortable communicating laterally with others who are on the same level as themselves. However, in order to make good decisions information needs to flow from the bottom, where decisions are implemented, up to the top where they are made in order to evaluate how well they work.

People tend to talk to others with whom they share space, who they are close to, who they have known for some time, who they see as similar, or who share the same interests. This is much like the way that people form relationships based on proximity, similarity, frequency, and intensity. They are more likely to communicate informally and share information because there is reduced uncertainty based on a common connection. This series of connections creates informal networks in the organization through which information flows. The activity of these informal networks can be a measure of how well the official networks are fulfilling the need for information.

We have a need for information and when it is not fulfilled, we seek out ways to fulfill it. Organizations have networks to communicate information to its members and much of the time these networks provide the information that is needed. However, there are times when they can become inadequate and do not provide the information people want, so they seek out other ways to get it through connections with others. This demand to fill the need for information to reduce uncertainty can motivate rumor and gossip.

The laws of uncertainty and shared meaning can motivate us to create and circulate rumor and gossip. When there is a lack of information, uncertainty is increased, so we seek to reduce it. When we experience something we may not fully understand, we can be motivated to make sense out of it by looking for shared meaning in it. These explanations have power because they can motivate people's behavior resulting in tangible consequences.

Organizational Climate

Organizational climate describes the nature of how people communicate with one another. It is important because it can affect people's state of mind. While it is mostly psychological in nature, it is communicated through the social interaction of people, so it can have tangible results manifested in their behavior. It is an important part of an organization because it can make us feel good about ourselves.

A positive climate makes an organization a fun place to be, motivating people to want to be a part of it. A negative climate can reduce an individual's commitment to the organization, so they feel less satisfied making them more likely to leave. Organizational climate is important because it affects the ability of people to work together and accomplish their desired outcomes. This is because it has an influence on the perceptions and expectations of themselves, others, and the organization.

Since climate is comprised of the social atmosphere within an organization, it is open to individual perceptions. People have a perception of the attitudes and emotions of others that may or may not be accurate. If people perceive others are feeling a certain way they may be more inclined to think that they should feel the same way too.

People have expectations about what type of climate they need to do their best work. This is often based upon their past experiences and personal preferences. Some people prefer a climate that is informal, fun, warm, friendly, and open to new ideas and information. Others may prefer a more fixed, formal, and structured climate that values tradition.

An organization's climate can have a great influence on its members' self-concept, which can affect their satisfaction and level of commitment to the group. If a climate is cold, formal, or overly negative it can hurt people's self-concept because it is affected by reflected feedback through the process of communicating.

If people are not receiving feedback that meets their needs, it can harm their self-concept making them less satisfied with the organization lowering their commitment and harming their ability to work effectively with others.

Organizational Culture

Organizational culture consists of the reoccurring patterns of communicating and behavior that comprise the rules and norms of interaction between individuals within an organization.

This can help facilitate the effective functioning of the organization because it reduces uncertainty by providing structure and stability. It is a means of sharing meaning to facilitate understanding of the organization and its members.

The culture of an organization serves a similar function as the culture of a country or geographic region. It can communicate its history, language, customs, rituals, and social reality. This can make becoming a new member of an organization feel like going to a foreign country. It's helpful for members of an organization to know its culture to increase their satisfaction, while fostering their commitment to it.

While organizational climate can change to reflect the emotional intensity of the moment, organizational culture changes more slowly over time. The culture often begins when an organization is created and develops in one of two ways. It can grow spontaneously through the natural interaction of its members over time through the process of behavioral reinforcement. Or, it can be created and developed intentionally to achieve specific desired outcomes. However, when a culture is imposed on an organization the members may try to create their own informal culture. By understanding how culture works, organizations can have options to develop a culture that is the most effective for them.

Organizational culture uses rules, norms, and other structural devices to motivate members to conform to its social reality. An organization's culture can help it to function effectively because without it people would not know how to behave or what was expected of them. Instead, they would do whatever they felt like doing increasing uncertainty making things chaotic.

Culture shares meaning between members so they can communicate and understand each other in order to accomplish their tasks. Culture helps to create common ground to develop the social connections that bring people together.

An important part of how we express culture is through rituals and traditions. Rituals are established patterns of communicating or behavior repeated in a similar way over time. They might involve the ways in which members interact and communicate with one another. They may involve regularly occurring activities such as coffee breaks or Monday morning meetings.

Traditions are patterns of behavior that an organization's members share based upon their mutual customs or beliefs. For example, an organization may believe strongly in supporting the families of its members, so they have events in which family members are encouraged to participate. Organizations may have rites of passage like having a party or ceremony when a person gets promoted, changes departments, or retires.

These activities reduce uncertainty because members get to know one another on a more personal level. When members participate in rituals and traditions together, it gives them a sense of unity of purpose and a feeling that everyone is in it together. This can be helpful in larger organizations where all members cannot feasibly get together at the same time. By participating in the same events, they can feel like they are part of the same community.

For example, when groups celebrate a holiday, they are unified in a common experience even though they may not all be physically together. These activities fulfill individual member's needs and wants for affiliation and recognition by creating connections between members that can increase their satisfaction and commitment to the organization.

In practically any culture there is the potential for splits or schisms that can divide it into smaller groups. This can lead to tension and competition for resources undermining the effectiveness of the organization. Members can have diverse interests motivating them to group themselves together based upon their interests or expertise.

A unique culture can develop around a particular specialization within the larger organization. Members are motivated to do this out of the need to associate with others who they perceive are like themselves to share interests they have in common. Members can be motivated to form informal groups just like they do in society based on familiarity, similarity, intensity, and proximity.

The most common way that people learn about an organization's culture is by experiencing it for themselves. This can take some time and they may make mistakes that can cause unnecessary tension. Organizations can make this process easier by providing a means to inform their members about how their culture works.

Organizational self-replication.

In many organizations there can be an internal inertia that resists change. This can be propagated by a self-replicating mechanism that works rather like cells in the human body. Our body replaces old cells with new ones that look the same as those they replace. If they were too different, our appearance would change and we would look like a different person.

People leave organizations and have to be replaced in order for it to survive. The people who select their replacements often self-replicate by hiring people just like those who left or who are like themselves.

The law of uncertainty motivates them to hire and promote people who are similar to those already in the organization. They hire them to reduce uncertainty, so they will support the existing culture because it promotes stability and security.

An organization is like other living organisms, it seeks to eliminate what it perceives as a threat. If new members are too different they could increase uncertainty that may pose a threat to the existing members.

Existing members may be reluctant to accept people they perceive as being too different, because if the new people think too differently, they could challenge the existing members' social reality creating tension.

If the new person's way of thinking prevails, the existing members might be perceived as being wrong undermining their power and authority potentially damaging their self-concept. This can provide motivation for organizations to avoid implementing change. This can be one reason why organizations can grow to a point where they cease to innovate and begin to stagnate, or decline.

If new members are too different than the existing members they may not fit in and could be ostracized, even rejected by the existing members. They might be creative or ambitious showing up existing members or making them look bad.

This could make some members feel that they are no longer effective and might loose their power or influence in the organization. This could motivate them to eliminate a threat they may perceive to their position by removing new members who might be considered too different.

If new members do not change to fit in, it could hurt their self-concept making them become dissatisfied and frustrated with the organization, so they may leave. They may feel pressure to change their behavior to fit in with the organization and its culture. If they change, then they may become just like the others and the people they replaced.

Organizational culture has the power to motivate people to conform because an organization can fulfill its members' needs and wants. It can also punish members who exhibit behavior outside acceptable norms forcing them to conform or leave. It is this process of self-replicating that can make an organization look virtually the same many years later. Having an awareness of this process means it does not necessarily have to hurt the organization.

There can be a characteristic of social reality whereby groups and individuals look to punish someone for the actions of others. There may be people who have committed transgressions that go unfettered until uncertainty becomes too high, then the group may need to restore balance by targeting an individual or group to be punished for the transgressions of everyone else.

This person is often innocent and undeserving of this treatment. They might be very accomplished, so others want them removed because they perceive them as a threat. They may be treated harshly, unfairly punished, even forced out. This could be characterized as the Crucifixion Principle.

Organizational Growth and Decline

Organizations go through the same developmental phases as groups and individual relationships because they are created by the connections between people. They can go through the process of creation, growth, maintenance, and decline. They can become successful and grow until they reach a point where the organization reaches a plateau, so growth and innovation declines and it goes out of business.

So, how can organizations be innovative and creative, grow successful, only to decline and wither away? The answer can be found in the laws of uncertainty, shared meaning, and investing.

When an organization is first created it is in the uncertainty reduction phase because there's a high degree of uncertainty. Uncertainty can work as a motivational influence if it is managed effectively. The people who comprise it are learning how to negotiate their roles, norms, rules, structure, and social reality.

They go through the process of behavioral reinforcement trying different things until they are accepted by others. At this point, there is a high degree of uncertainty, so they are possibly the most open they can be to new ideas and new ways of doing things. This flexibility helps them to be innovative and creative fostering success.

When an organization becomes older and larger, chances are good that they have significantly reduced uncertainty. They have solidified their roles, norms, rules, structure, and social reality. Rather than changing these things, members are expected to conform to the organization's ways of doing things. People with different ideas may be cast as troublemakers to be ignored or removed.

Reduced uncertainty provides security and stability, however, it also reduces the flexibility and the ability to adapt to change. It can create an attitude of, "I know what I'm doing," which can lead to arrogance. Arrogance is one of the leading causes of organizational decline because it reduces awareness and options.

In a new organization, reduced uncertainty is followed by the shared meaning phase of development. As most of the members are new, they're involved in the process of sharing meaning about themselves, others, and the organization. They negotiate what the organization stands for and what it means to be a member.

Since this is a process that is fluid and evolving, it's open to change and interpretation. As an organization grows and becomes larger, it has more established shared meanings between its members about the organization and what it means to be a member. Members have less ability to contribute to changing that meaning, and are instead expected to conform to it. Members who share different meanings about the organization are more likely to change to fit in or leave.

When an organization is new, members usually have very little invested in it because the organization has not yet developed. It is less likely to have established much structure or hierarchies that can create value in organizations.

This means that the members are more flexible and willing to try different approaches to become effective and successful because there is less investment to lose. Structure is developed to help increase stability, but it can also restrict innovation and trying new things that could be successful.

When an organization goes through the investing phase of development, its members can become more cautious about what they do because they do not want to loose the time, energy, and other resources they have invested in it. This can make them less likely to innovate or do things differently because doing so could be perceived as increasing uncertainty.

There are often hierarchies and ranks created by the members because they have invested significant amounts of their time there. They are likely to resist change and innovation because they do not want to lose their investment, power, benefits, or place in the organization.

The process of communicating will change as an organization grows. In the beginning, it is generally smaller so members can communicate with everyone in the organization more frequently regardless of rank. Information at the bottom can more easily flow to the top where decisions are made.

There's less apprehension about communicating across the organization because it is smaller and everybody is closer, physically as well as psychologically. It is more likely that everyone is all in one location sharing the same space. This encourages communicating networks to facilitate the flow of information needed to innovate and grow.

In larger organizations, members are less likely to communicate across the organization because it is more difficult and can be perceived as increasing uncertainty. The organization's culture may even discourage it. Instead, there are often established formal communicating networks members are expected to use.

They can be more distant, often physically separated by offices, different floors, perhaps even different locations. They may be reluctant to share their ideas for fear of rejection, punishment, or the loss of their investment.

Members are more likely to communicate with others on the same level or in the same department. This can reduce the flow of information that could help them be innovative and creative, by reducing their awareness leading to poorer decisions. This can encourage some to use information as a means to improve their own position rather than the organization.

Organizations have their own needs and wants, just as individuals do. When an organization is starting out it has lots of needs and wants, but it likely has few resources to fulfill them. This motivates the members to do more with less. It encourages them to come up with new and creative ways of doing things in order to save resources, like time and money.

As an organization grows larger, it can attract more resources, but there still is a problem of allocation. In order to receive the resources they need, members are more likely to conform to the expectations of those who provide the resources, rather than develop their own means of accomplishing a task. They are more likely to be less innovative and creative. They can be less likely to question their superiors and just do what they're told.

When an organization is new, the members utilize the social reality of society or their past experiences. They may share different social realities that can create uncertainty about the organization and what to expect. As it grows, members negotiate what the social reality of the organization will eventually become.

This means that to some extent they have a say in what the organization will look like, how it behaves, how it communicates, and what it does. This can provide more flexibility to create an organization that is highly receptive not only to its members, but also to its customers and the outside environment.

As an organization grows its social reality solidifies, so individual members have less say in what that means. It can also become more resistant to outside influences. This means that it could potentially develop a bunker type mentality where it not only does not accommodate change, it actually resists it.

This can be expressed when they say things like, "That's the way we have always done it." This can make the organization less flexible to respond to changing circumstances necessary for it to function effectively.

Uncertainty and Organizational Communicating

What would happen if you no longer belonged to any groups or organizations? Many well-known people have spent time alone on their own, outside the influence of others. Jesus spent forty days fasting in the desert. Buddha was thought to have spent forty nine days sitting under a tree to find enlightenment and spiritual insight. Other people have gone on spiritual quests or spent time in the wilderness, both physically and mentally.

So, if you could get away from all the groups that influence you, what would you do? What new insights could you gain about yourself, others, and the world around you? Would you read, develop a new skill, travel, or sit under a tree?

While we may not be able to get away from others for that long, we can find some time to get away from the influence of groups or organizations. It could be for a week or a weekend.

Having some time away from groups and organizations can help us increase our awareness of how they influence us. This can help us reflect on what things are working well and what we would like to change. Groups and organizations provide us with many benefits, but we can also spend some time on our own. Doing this can help us to relax, reduce stress, and process information to help us clear our mind to become more effective.

We can develop our skills, clarify our perceptions, and manage our expectations to make them more realistic and helpful. We can evaluate our needs and wants, and how well they are being met. We can sharpen our awareness and find more effective options.

We can simplify our life by focusing on our desired outcomes and what is really important to us. We can spend time without worrying about meeting the expectations of others.

Some groups seem to get along and things go well, so we don't think much about them. Other times nothing seems to work leaving us feeling frustrated. Groups and organizations can utilize the laws of uncertainty, shared meaning, and investing as a methodological tool to help diagnose problems and find solutions to make them more effective.

By understanding the law of uncertainty, groups and organizations can balance uncertainty with uncertainty reduction to provide stability, yet motivate effective behaviors to foster innovation and avoid becoming stagnant. The law of shared meaning can be used to create a common culture and positive climate that fosters effective roles and norms.

Understanding the law of investing and how it motivates behavior can help to make groups and organizations more effective. It can help encourage member satisfaction and commitment. These laws can be utilized to fulfill needs and wants, manage perceptions and expectations, and help us to achieve our desired outcomes.

Chapter 7
Societal Communicating

Societal communicating is the fourth and final level of interaction. It is about how we communicate with others in public and how others communicate with us in society. Societal communicating is comprised of several different methods of communicating including how people communicate with others in public, how others communicate publicly with you, and how we as a society communicate.

Societal communicating consists of the ways we make connections to communicate our Great Idea with others in society. It could be to a few people or to large audiences. It can include written messages like a memo, email, letter, report, article, or book. It can be verbal like a speech, presentation, or video. It can involve the use of technology that is controlled by others like television, radio, or the internet.

In most forms of communicating, you create your Great Idea and make a direct connection with people you know who can provide you with feedback. In public communicating, we are less likely to communicate directly with people we know.

We are more likely to make an indirect connection through a third party to others we cannot see and do not know. We may receive direct feedback, delayed feedback, or no feedback at all.

Societal communicating often utilizes technology, which can create a disconnect between us and our audience making it more difficult to facilitate feedback. Public communicating tends to be more formal, structured, and planned in advance, before the audience actually receives it. This means that in public communicating, it is helpful to know how to structure and communicate messages to achieve your desired outcome.

Most of the time when we communicate with others, we use the third style of communicating described earlier. This is a conversational style of communicating that provides instantaneous feedback. In public communicating, this happens when we speak in front of an audience or give a group presentation.

We can read their facial expressions and see their eye contact to ascertain their interest or attentiveness. There may be an opportunity for people to ask questions to provide us with feedback. Through feedback we can know more about our audience and how we are being perceived by them.

Societal communicating has the potential increase uncertainty because we don't always know how our message will be received by the public. We don't always know who our audience is or receive feedback from them. People can use the power of the law of uncertainty by publicly communicating misinformation or withholding information. This can increase uncertainty undermining stability motivating behavior with potentially negative consequences.

Much of how we share meaning to construct social reality takes place through public communicating. It is the means by which people share stories about ourselves and others to create a common culture. We can share meaning through creative expression in the arts and entertainment.

Public communicating can give society a sense of collective identity making us feel like we belong and are connected to others. It gives us a sense of what it means to be a member of society. It is how we share rituals, traditions, and communal values. It helps us to define who we are as individuals and as a society.

Sharing information through public communicating is essential for people to invest in themselves, others, and in society. This is important because it provides the information we need to make decisions, accomplish tasks, and achieve desired outcomes.

Individuals communicate in public in order to encourage others to invest in them and their ideas. This process is necessary to facilitate creativity, invention, exploration, discovery, and self expression that are necessary for society to function and grow.

Society and Social Reality.

Throughout history many societies have risen and fallen. Some became great while others never developed. Some still have an influence on us today hundreds, even thousands of years later. Some became great for only a short time while others existed for hundreds of years. Great societies throughout history have shifted geographic locations around the world.

So, how does a society make great advances only to fall into decline? Consideration has been given to pivotal moments in history, prominent individuals, discoveries, inventions, and the availability of natural resources.

The power of social reality can be a significant motivating force that influences the development of society. Social reality is driven by the law of uncertainty because it motivates people's behavior exerting pressures to conform as a means of social control to cope with physical reality. It does this by creating expectations of what is acceptable behavior, enforced with rewards and punishments.

Social reality can be a positive force encouraging people to develop new ideas, inspire creativity, encourage innovation, motivate people to take action, and communicate ideas with one another.

Examining how uncertainty drives innovation and creativity can help us understand how to improve society and our quality of life. The process of communicating can be applied to examining the means by which people's ideas become reality.

Discoveries and inventions are facilitated by the social reality we share because there first has to be the right conditions to encourage people to think differently about things and then communicate their Great Idea to others. Innovation can create a great society when social reality encourages people to develop new ideas and new ways of doing things to make them a reality.

Throughout history, changes in social reality have changed the nature of society. In the Middle Ages, social reality was based on The Church and religious texts of the past. This social reality was changed by The Reformation and The Renaissance. Changes in social reality allowed the introduction of the scientific method, which created of new knowledge through research. This resulted in changes in physical reality that were so useful in advancing society they are still utilized today.

When an idea is communicated and shares meaning with the members of a society it is more likely to become a reality. This makes the conceptual process that precedes the creation of physical reality especially important. How information like your Great Idea is communicated through connections between people can determine how it can manifest itself in physical reality. Advancements in society are motivated by the law of uncertainty because it makes people look beyond what they already know to understand what they don't know.

How society reduces uncertainty can be a critical factor in how that society advances and if it becomes a great society or not. There have been many ideas and inventions that existed as a Great Idea long before social reality allowed them to gain the acceptance necessary to become a reality. People refer to this when they say things like, it was ahead of its time.

Excessive uncertainty can be detrimental for society. If uncertainty is too high, people may be less able to get things done because they are more concerned about their own safety and stability. This can discourage people from investing in one another or themselves. Conversely, excessive uncertainty reduction can also be detrimental because it can lead to arrogance and overconfidence creating a lack of awareness. It can remove the motivation to act and do things that increased uncertainty would provide.

Excessive uncertainty reduction can be harmful when everything is decided at the top such as by government. It reduces the motivation for innovation and creation by inhibiting people's motivation to take action to do things. This is why some forms of government such as socialist, communist, and authoritarian cease to function effectively and often fail because they have reduced some types of uncertainty to a point that it inhibits innovation by reducing the motivation for people to develop new ideas and ways of doing things.

Advancements in society are driven by the law of shared meaning because it facilitates the creation and dissemination of ideas between people. Societies that are able to share meaning to encourage understanding, foster creativity, and promote innovation because they share a sense of common identity and commitment.

However, if a society is unable to share meaning, it can inhibit them from communicating with one another and creating a shared social reality. This might happen when they do not share a common language or common culture. When people have difficulty communicating with one another, society can become fragmented creating competing social realities.

When a society becomes removed from the social reality that made it great, it can begin to fragment leading to competing factions that can cause it to deteriorate. When increasing numbers of people become more disconnected, they are less able to communicate or share meaning.

When people have fewer connections with one another, social reality can break down hastening its decline. When segments of society try to impose their specialized version of social reality on others, it can lead to societal fragmentation, which can undermine a great society so it declines and decays.

Cultural Societal Reality

An important function of societal communicating is to create and maintain a common culture. Culture is a specialized version of social reality created by groups of people over time to reduce uncertainty about themselves and the world around them. It is a means to share meaning through customs, traditions, behaviors, and ways of communicating. Culture is something that we are all born into and that we all have, making it inevitable and unavoidable.

Culture often originates in a particular geographic area and can be associated with a specific group of people based on their shared history and experiences. They often communicate their culture through their appearance and what they say and do. Culture influences many aspects of life including art, music, literature, clothing, religion, and architecture.

Culture is a significant part of our lives because it shapes how we communicate and how we interact with others. It contains its own social reality consisting of norms of behavior and patterns of communicating. It is important to have an awareness of how culture motivates behavior.

Culture creates security through rules that are often institutionalized in laws. It creates power and authority that is communicated through levels of hierarchy. It has its own networks of connections through which people communicate. It reduces uncertainty by communicating important aspects of life so that people can better understand themselves and others.

Practically anywhere we live, we communicate with people from other cultures. Understanding other cultures enriches our lives by looking at familiar things in new and different ways. Other cultures have faced the similar problems and have approached them in different ways. Understanding culture helps us to avoid misunderstandings that can lead to unnecessary tension or conflict. It can help us see things from other people's point of view.

Culture helps to reduce uncertainty because it tells us who we are, our history, our values, and how things came to be the way they are today. When we meet someone for the first time we look to reduce uncertainty about them, so we utilize information about culture based upon our past experiences to make inferences about them. Culture can also increase uncertainty when we meet others from a culture we know little about because we do not know what to expect from them.

Culture is a manifestation of the law of shared meaning. It is how we share meaning about who we are with large groups of people. People invest shared meaning in art, music, and food based on their culture. People who share the same culture often participate in similar rituals and traditions.

Culture invests symbols as well as objects with meaning. It is a means by which we give our experiences a deeper significance. Cultures can develop their own unique ways of communicating to share meaning through language, which is often associated with a specific group of people and geographic area.

Culture provides a means of investing in others without having to know them personally. When people share a culture, they know many things about one another because they share a similar social reality. This helps provide a connection to create and maintain relationships.

When people move to another place, like a foreign country, they often group together in communities with others from the same culture. They may even move to areas that look similar or have a similar climate and terrain. People of different cultures may find it difficult to form relationships and invest in one another because they perceive the cultural differences as increasing uncertainty rather than looking for connections they have in common.

Culture is usually associated with geographic affiliation. Geographic affiliation is a geographic area that people have an attachment to giving it a deeper meaning. It could be a country, state, city, or region. It is a place they feel a connection to, are from, live now, or have ancestors. People may feel a connection to a culture and to the geographic area associated with it.

Geographic affiliation can play an important part in the development of a culture because culture can be shaped by its typography, landscape, plants, animals, climate, and natural resources. People are likely to live there, but they do not have to have actually been there.

Cultures develop their own individual characteristics based on the natural resources that were available to them. They used local resources to make food, clothing, and homes creating their own distinctive style. People took inspiration from their surroundings for art and music.

Geographic affiliation often determines how people fulfill their needs and wants creating culture. People everywhere have similar needs and wants to fulfill, but they have found many different ways to fulfill them as expressed in different cultures.

Culture is not only associated with nationalities and geographic regions, it can also be a part of groups and organizations. Culture is a way of characterizing a group's social reality including its norms of behavior and how people communicate with one another. It affects how people share meaning about themselves, others, and the world around them. It determined how they respond to physical reality.

Large groups of people, such as an organization or nation, can develop subcultures. These are smaller groups of people that can be a part of a larger culture, but share stronger connections and common characteristics. They often share a specialized version of social reality. These subcultures can be affiliated by geographic area, political or religious beliefs, gender, professions, hobbies, activities, and personal interests.

People have many of the same needs and wants, but different cultures have devised different ways to fulfill them. Many of the ways that we fulfill our needs and wants are identified with culture. Learning about how different cultures approach the same problems in different ways helps us to look at what is familiar to us in new and different ways.

Everyone needs food, clothing, and shelter to survive, but they can fulfill these needs in different ways. Many cultures are known for their unique type of foods that are based on its history and traditions using locally available ingredients. Clothing styles are based upon a culture's needs, climate, history, and available raw materials. Architectural styles are based upon a culture's social reality using locally available materials.

Culture shapes how we perceive uncertainty and how we reduce it. It is the expression of a collective shared meaning. It determines how we invest in others and society. It provides perspective on how to interpret people's experiences. It influences perceptions making it a powerful force because it motivates behavior and how people communicate.

Culture invests behavior with meaning, so people of different cultures can have different interpretations of the same kinds of things making it a source of misunderstanding, tension, or conflict.

In order to reduce uncertainty we often make inferences about people based upon their culture from information we have gathered in the past. Even though this information may be outdated or inaccurate, we do this in order to reduce uncertainty. When we do not check if our perceptions are accurate, it can lead to generalizations such as stereotypes that could give us a false impression of someone before we get to know them.

Culture is an expression of social reality, so we may not be aware of how much it affects us. It is helpful to have an awareness of our own culture as well as how others differ. By being more aware of other cultures we gain a respect for them as well as an appreciation of our own.

Diversity tends to be approached in terms of the differences that make us unique. Emphasizing differences can increase uncertainty and advance generalizations or stereotypes by emphasizing how we are different. By thinking about culture in a new way, we can look for commonalities to make connections with others so uncertainty can be reduced. Cultural should not create division, but create connections that bring us closer together by emphasizing the similarities that can create shared meanings with others.

We do this to reduce uncertainty about one another, so we can get to know each other better to form relationships. We can utilize the law of shared meaning to understand more about each other as well as ourselves. We can make connections to share meaning with others to understand them better to create common ground.

We invest in others to develop relationships with them. While we are culturally different, we are similar in that we seek to fulfill similar needs and wants, and achieve mutual desired outcomes. Rather than adapting to a culture by imitating what others do, we can create understanding to develop a culture that we share.

People of all cultures join groups and organizations in order to fulfill needs and wants, form relationships, and achieve desired outcomes. These are things everyone has in common that can encourage them to make connections to help them understand each other's culture.

When people spend time together, they utilize self-disclosure to reduce uncertainty about one another creating connections to build trust. And when they do, they feel safe and secure enough to invest in relationships with one another, in organizations, and in society.

Conflict

The word conflict has been used to describe everything from a disagreement to war. Conflict is often a result of the increased uncertainty. It can happen when there is uncertainty about tasks, rules, norms, responsibilities, desired outcomes, or how resources are allocated.

When a desired outcome is unclear it creates a higher degree of uncertainty about what to do and who should do it. We look for meaning in people's behavior to explain why they start conflicts and what they really hope to gain from them.

We invest conflict itself with meaning often characterizing it in negative terms. While conflict often carries negative connotations, if managed effectively it can have positive outcomes.

The law of investing motivates us to invest in other people, in groups, and in society. However, there are times when we might feel that our investment is threatened. Conflict often involves allocation of resources and competing interests because we have limited resources to satisfy potentially unlimited needs and wants.

This can create conflict over how those needs and wants are fulfilled. Conflict often happens because there is something at stake. People can be motivated to disagree or create conflict because they feel that they have something invested and conflict is how they can get what they want. Or they may create conflict in order to protect their investment because they feel that they are losing something.

Two communicating skills that are helpful in a conflict are awareness and options. Just as we have our own individual style of communicating, we have our own approach to conflict. It can be helpful to increase your awareness of how you usually approach conflict.

We may jump to conclusions, make assumptions, get angry, or retaliate. While this is a natural tendency, improving our awareness helps us to know how we are coming across to others, so that we can take a more positive and constructive approach. This gives us more options to increase the chances for resolution.

Conflict can have an intensity that brings out emotional responses that makes us react less rationally resulting in unintended or undesired outcomes. It can be helpful in conflict situations to take a moment and pause to consider your desired outcome. Is your desired outcome to escalate the situation and perhaps damage the relationship, or is it to work out a reasonable solution?

By pausing for a moment to consider your desired outcome, you can reduce the emotional intensity of the situation to increase your awareness and consider your options. By not responding to others with the same intensity, you do not give them a reason to continue to fight. Instead, they are encouraged to talk about the issues improving the chances for resolution.

We have all experienced conflict, so it can be helpful to look at it in a new way. While we all want to get our way in a conflict, the reality is that we can't get it all of the time. Sometimes we get what we want and other times we don't. Then there are those conflicts that never seem to go away, so we need to find a way to manage them.

Just as we consider the effectiveness of how we communicate, consider the effectiveness of resolving conflict. This helps to avoid thinking in terms like good or bad and win or lose, so we can find something positive in a conflict even if we don't achieve our desired outcome. This does not mean that the issues are necessary resolved the way we would like, but instead the tension surrounding them is resolved or at least reduced.

Conflict is often perceived as something bad to be avoided. We often think that conflicts are something we should not be proud of because it is a personal shortcoming or failing. For the most part these perceptions are not true. Conflict can be constructive or destructive regardless of whether we get what we want or not.

It can be constructive when it utilizes effective communicating skills because it helps reduce uncertainty, share meaning, invest in others, and gain new insights in order to achieve something better than they might have accomplished individually.

Conflict can be harmful when it inhibits us from gaining new insights and information. It can increase uncertainty when it prevents us from changing or finding new ways of doing things that might be better. It can be harmful when it damages our self-concept or hurts our relationships.

It can be frustrating when conflict prevents effective problem solving or reaching the best possible solution or desired outcome. By understanding how we communicate about conflict, we can minimize its harmful affects and focus on the helpful ones.

Working together in difficult circumstances can bring people closer together. This is because shared experiences can create meanings that strengthen relationships. Whether the outcome is positive or not, working through conflict can make people feel more connected.

People are motivated by the law of shared meaning to talk about their experiences with others because it helps invest them with meaning. By working through a conflict together, people can develop trust so that they are more likely to invest in others in the future.

Crisis

A critical part of societal communicating is how people communicate during a crisis because it can make the difference between success or failure. A crisis is usually based around an event or series of events that causes a sudden and extreme shock or change.

A crisis dramatically increases the level of uncertainty undermining our stability, security, and even safety. It has the potential to cause emotional as well as physical harm.

A crisis often takes priority over everything else until it is resolved. It forces us to make decisions and confront issues we might otherwise avoid or may not even know about.

Crisis is a physical manifestation of the law of uncertainty. It is characterized by a sudden and extreme increase in uncertainty motivating us to take immediate action. It can undermine our feelings of safety and security increasing uncertainty long after the crisis has passed.

The law of shared meaning motivates us to look for meaning in the things that happen to us. We invest them with meaning in order to make sense out of them and to reduce uncertainty. We want to know why things happen because it gives us a deeper understanding of ourselves, others, and the world around us.

The nature of a crisis can be affected by our perception of social reality. A crisis usually involves events that happen in physical reality that we react to based upon how we construct social reality. Crisis can be more than just physical, it is often psychological as well.

We want to make sense of or experiences, so we invest them with meaning to help us know what to do about them. How we utilize social reality to interpret a crisis can make a difference in how successfully we negotiate it. How we utilize social reality to interpret our experiences can have consequences in physical reality.

Phases of crisis communicating.

Crisis can be overwhelming, but it can be easier to cope with if we approach it as a series of phases. We can learn from our experiences and gain new knowledge to help us handle a crisis better in the future.

1. The law of uncertainty phase. A crisis can begin with a rapid and dramatic increase in uncertainty undermining our stability and security. Everyone involved is aware of the crisis. It often overwhelms their resources and normal methods of problem solving.

Just what constitutes a crisis may be difficult to define, but everyone involved knows when one happens. There is often a limited amount of time to respond because the longer it takes, the more serious the consequences may be. Circumstances change the normal ways of doing things for everyone involved which may continue once the crisis has passed.

Much of what constitutes a crisis depends upon how we perceive and interpret events. What may be a crisis for one person may not for others. How we do this is often based upon our past experiences and skills. A crisis can create feelings of anxiety, anger, or fear because we may not know what to do or what will happen next. This can motivate people to take action to restore stability.

2. The law of shared meaning phase. When everyone involved is aware of the crisis, they begin communicating about it. They invest what is happening with shared meaning recognizing it as a crisis. The need to communicate dramatically increases to the point where it may overwhelm us.

When people communicate, they characterize the crisis in terms that are negative or positive. How people communicate about the crisis in its early stages can affect their perception of what is happening to them shaping their expectations. These perceptions and expectations motivate behavior because they can have tangible consequences. How people communicate at this stage can manifest itself in physical reality, affecting how successful the outcome will be.

Negative messages can increase emotional intensity by increasing uncertainty. They increase the perception of negative circumstances, which can create expectations that things are going badly causing people to become apprehensive or even panic, diminishing their ability to react effectively to their circumstances. Negative messages can increase uncertainty undermining people's confidence making them less likely to do what is necessary in a crisis, which could make things worse.

Communicating positive messages provides information to help give people confidence to do what is necessary in a crisis. This emphasizes stability so that people will remain calm helping them to think clearly to resolve the problem. Positive messages can help to decrease emotional intensity by reducing uncertainty.

They show support for others to bolster their confidence increasing their chances of success. If people have the perception that the crisis is something they can handle, they may expect things to work out giving them the confidence to handle them more effectively.

As difficult as it may be in times of crisis, it is helpful to communicate some positive messages emphasizing the ways we can resolve the situation. It is helpful to communicate these messages because they reduce uncertainty, build stability, reduce anxiety, and invest in relationships.

Having a balanced distribution of positive and negative messages can have a beneficial affect on our perceptions and expectations. When our perceptions are improved, it can improve our expectations, so we will feel better about our situation. Doing this can give us added confidence to act more confidently, so we can feel more assured about the situation, which can help to resolve things more positively.

When we stay positive we can feel better about ourselves and our ability to do our best to achieve the best possible outcome under the circumstances and overcome adversity. This does not mean that we should be unrealistic or characterize the situation as being more positive than it actually is, but not just focus on the negative. A crisis can make us think in new ways, gain new skills, and challenge ourselves in ways we might otherwise not do.

3. The law of investing phase. A crisis is an overwhelming increase in uncertainty that motivates people to take action to return to a normal, stable state. Eventually the level of uncertainty reaches a peak or turning point where it begins to subside either naturally or through the efforts of people to resolve it.

Negative messages should be diminishing and positive messages should be increasing as people shift their attention from the crisis itself to what needs to be done afterwards. The emotional intensity should drop as people begin to feel a sense of relief that the worst is over.

In this phase, we seek to restore the previous state of normality or if that's not possible establish a new state of equilibrium. Because a crisis overwhelms old norms or ways of doing things, we can be motivated to find new ways of doing things to resolve the crisis. One of the positive aspects of crisis is that it gets people to think about what is familiar to them in new ways.

We look at the causes, at what worked, and what didn't work to resolve it. New norms and skills that helped to resolve the crisis can be kept. We can learn from our experience to take a bad thing and turn it around to make it better. Even in bad situations, it can be helpful to look for the good things that we can benefit from.

It can take time to come to terms with a crisis because it takes time to fit the new information in with what we already know. We may need time to think about things or process our experiences because we tend to perceive things based upon past experience that can make some things difficult to assimilate or utilize.

This works like the perception process where we select, organize, and interpret the information we perceive to fit it in with what we already know so it can be useful to us. We do this to fit present reality into our own personal version of social reality, which is based upon our perceptions of past experiences. The degree to which we are able to process this information determines how well adjusted we are with the experience to improve our response in the future.

A crisis can increase uncertainty to the point where we question everything we know and believe in. So, we need to take time to process new information to fit it in with what we already know and past experiences. It's like the books in the library. If there is an earthquake, and all the books fall on the floor, they have to be re-shelved in the proper order, which takes time. Similarly, our experiences need to be processed and reordered in order to shape our version of social reality.

4. After a crisis. How we feel after a crisis can have a significant affect on our self-concept. If we feel that things went as well as they could, it can improve our self-concept making us feel confident about our abilities. If we feel that the crisis has not been effectively resolved or things could have gone better, it can hurt our self-concept. By evaluating our skills before and after a crisis, we can be better prepared for what may happen in the future.

Once uncertainty has been reduced to tolerable levels, we may try to establish a stable set of norms. However, things may not return to how they were before, but instead there will be a new state of normality to create stability. The difference can be determined by the severity of the crisis and how much it forced us to make changes.

Many of the ways that things were done during the crisis may become a part of the new state of normality. In a crisis, we can learn new ways of doing things, making decisions, obtaining information, using resources, and making connections with others for support. It can motivate us to make changes we may have wanted to make, but had put off because they seemed too uncertain.

If a crisis passes relatively quickly people are more likely to return to norms more similar to those utilized before the crisis because they are familiar. If a crisis drags on, they are more likely to get accustomed to the changes crisis brings making them less likely to return to the norms they had before the crisis. If it takes a long time to reduce uncertainty, they will become more accustomed to the new norms.

Crisis, like conflict, can have positive outcomes. It shows us where our methods of doing things are inadequate. It can make us do things differently and develop new solutions. It can make us gather new information and seek out support from others. It can make us learn new things and try new approaches that we normally might not have considered. Many of the safety measures and training programs we have today originated from what people learned from responding to crises.

Changing Social Reality

The story of the Tower of Babel tells how the whole earth was of one language and the people were one. Nothing was restrained from them and what they imagined to do. Nothing they planned to do was impossible for them.

In response, God confounded their language, so they would not understand one another and scattered them all over the earth. Now, they were no longer able to work together and did mistrust one another. When people share a common social reality they can foster creation and innovation. When it fragments, society can cease to function as effectively.

In order for a society to function, people must be able to communicate with others. They need to build trust in order to invest their resources in each other and in society. One of the mechanisms that allows people to do this is social reality. When there is a clear unified social reality, society has a basis for making the connections that helps it to function effectively.

However, as society developed people engaged in increasing role specialization. While this can be helpful in furthering the development of specialized expertise, people are more likely to spend increasing amounts of their time communicating only with people who are like themselves to the point where they no longer have connections with people outside their network. This has the potential to make society fragmented.

For instance, there was a time when the majority of people lived in rural farming communities. They shared similar experiences and communicated about things that were familiar to them creating a shared social reality. Most of their social reality was created by communicating directly with people who they knew. They had the knowledge and skills to be self-reliant, fulfilling many of their needs and wants in their own communities.

This self-reliance helped them make it through the Great Depression and win two World Wars. As times changed, more people moved to the cities and suburbs, worked in increasingly specialized jobs, and got the things they needed from others like from a store. They became less self-reliant becoming increasingly dependent on a system where others provide almost everything needed for their survival. This changed their social reality.

Social reality can potentially change in two ways, people change it or events change it for them. Throughout history there have been many pivotal moments that have changed social reality affecting people's behavior.

A few of these include the rise of Ancient Greece, the fall of Rome, the Magna Carta, the Reformation, the Renaissance, and self determination embodied in the American Revolution. It is through people's experiences that help build culture providing the basis for shared meaning that forms social reality.

The law of uncertainty has a way of changing social reality. Sometimes it can happen abruptly, while other times it happens more subtly with change going practically unnoticed. One method of change is through a crisis.

In a crisis, people make changes to adapt to their new circumstances in order to restore economic equilibrium. The Great Depression was an economic and agricultural crisis that motivated people to change their behavior in order to survive.

The longer a crisis persists, the more likely changes will become comfortable making a return to past ways more uncomfortable after the crisis ends. Returning to the ways of the past can be perceived as increasing uncertainty because they may be perceived as having contributed to creating the crisis. If the new behaviors helped alleviate the crisis, then they will be perceived as reducing uncertainty and are more likely to be kept.

The Depression was a long term crisis that motivated the behavior of the people it affected for a very long time after it was over, creating a social reality of hard work and saving that still exists today.

If a society does not share meaning through common experiences that they invest with meaning, then two or more competing social realities could develop. While society is motivated by the law of uncertainty to create social reality, there can be two or more competing social realities. When a society has competing social realities, it has the potential to become divided.

For instance, the nature of social reality would significantly change again during the 1960's with the Vietnam War, which was another long term crisis. Instead of uniting society with a single social reality, it would divide society creating two competing social realities. Many decades later this legacy has manifested itself in the liberal and conservative divide in society.

Since then, no one single shared social reality has fully emerged to replace the one of the Great Depression and the World Wars. Intervening events fractured the old social realities creating several competing new ones.

Conservatism and liberalism are two well known versions of social reality. When there are two or more competing social realities there needs to be a release of the tension that is created. Social reality does not develop overnight. It can take years, perhaps decades for it to manifest itself in physical reality.

Social reality has changed in the past, so it will change in the future. When the existing social reality changes, what will take its place? Since the law of uncertainty motivates us to take action or events will make us change, if this tension is not resolved there is a high likelihood of a crisis occurring to change social reality again.

Uncertainty and Society

In order to reduce uncertainty about the future, much time and effort has been expended in the planning, researching, even portraying what the future might be like both in reality and in works of fiction. We are motivated to know more about the future even though much of what is predicted doesn't actually happen.

We are familiar with predictions of driving hover cars and flying in jet packs. People would live under the ocean and take vacations on the moon. Yet, many of these predictions didn't materialize. Many events that increased uncertainty were not foreseen like the fall of the Soviet Union, terrorism, and the financial crises.

We make plans for the future, however, by doing this we may be planning based on certainty. Many times we have seen planning for the future fail resulting in unexpected and undesired outcomes.

Utilizing the law of uncertainty to evaluate the future relies more on how needs and wants motivate behavior. It can be helpful to consider how the law of uncertainty will motivate behavior and shape social reality in the future, just as it has shaped and changed society in the past.

In scientific research, a hypothesis is formulated and then is tested to prove its validity. If it cannot be disproven, it can be considered to be true. The laws of uncertainty, shared meaning, and investing were applied to virtually all aspects of behavioral communicating in order to find an area where they did not apply or where they did not hold true. Such a case was not found affirming their validity.

The laws of uncertainty, shared meaning, and investing have demonstrated the potential to provide a unified explanation of the nature of human behavior and communicating. The law of uncertainty suggests that on a deeper level there is an underlying chaotic state that creates the energy that runs society. These laws have the potential to be useful as an analytical methodology in many fields.

Much of human activity throughout history has been motivated by the law of uncertainty. The pursuit of reducing uncertainty should have resulted in a significant decrease in the amount of uncertainty people experience. However, in recent years more people have experienced greater uncertainty than ever before.

The last two centuries have seen more advancement in daily life than ever before in history. Yet, today most people are dependent on others to fulfill most of their needs and wants, with many things coming from outside of their community, even from the other side of the globe. People used to be more self-reliant for many of their needs and wants, with most of them fulfilled in their own community.

Society has created many institutions to reduce uncertainty, however, they are subject to many of the forces described in this book. As society changes people create structures, bureaucracies, and hierarchies that become rigid making them vulnerable to uncertainty.

This means the next great crisis is not a question of if it will happen, but when, and how devastating will it be. If we understand the power of the law of uncertainty, we can mitigate its negative effects and find the positive ones. So, how ready will we be for future uncertainty and the next great crisis?

Despite society's efforts over thousands of years to reduce uncertainty, never before in the history of mankind have so many people been so thoroughly affected by uncertainty. Society has made great advancements to reduce uncertainty, but has our progress also made us more vulnerable to the law of uncertainty?

Perhaps, the more complicated our systems become, the more vulnerable they are to uncertainty. Perhaps we should be looking at building social institutions to foster independence and self-reliance in order to flow with uncertainty rather than try to control it.

Life is uncertain. The world can be chaotic. We don't know what the future holds for us. The purpose of this book is to explore how uncertainty affects us because it is always present. It influences how we think and motivates our behavior.

Throughout history, most of human activity has been motivated by uncertainty. It affects all of us and most everything in our lives. This makes it a topic that is difficult to cover in one book. It is a topic that could be examined and discussed for some time to come. So, this book focuses on how uncertainty affects how we communicate and our behavior.

This is not meant to be the last word on uncertainty, but instead a beginning. It is meant to increase awareness in order to provide a place to initiate a discussion of how uncertainty affects us all.

In an increasingly interconnected world, how do we protect ourselves from the potential affects of increasing uncertainty? While we may never fully control or even understand the nature of uncertainty one thing is certain, absolute uncertainty will be a part of our lives now and in the future.

HH
Heather Hill